Negotiation Strategy for Lawyers

XAVIER M. FRASCOGNA, JR.

Xavier M. Frascogna, Jr., is a partner in the Jackson, Mississippi, law firm of Frascogna & Brasfield. He received his B.A. and M.A. from Mississippi State University, J.D. (with distinction) from Mississippi College. He also received an M.B.A. and M.S.S. from Mississippi College, and is a member of the Mississippi bar.

Frascogna is a member of the American Bar Association, holding membership in its Forum Committee on the Entertainment and Sports Industries. He serves as an adjunct professor of law at Mississippi College School of Law teaching courses in negotiation.

Frascogna is co-author of *Successful Artist Management* published in 1979 by Billboard Publications. The book, which deals with the business, legal, and creative aspects of career development in the entertainment industry, was nominated for an American Bar Association "Gavel" Award and was the recipient of a 1980 "ASCAP—Deems Taylor" Book Award.

H. LEE HETHERINGTON

H. Lee Hetherington lives in Los Angeles, California, where he is Vice President, Administration and Finance for Columbia Pictures Television. Hetherington received his B.A. from Millsaps College, a J.D. from the University of Mississippi School of Law, and an LL.M. with a concentration in the field of Trade Regulation from New York University School of Law. He is admitted to the bar in New York and Mississippi.

Hetherington is a member of the American Bar Association, holding membership in the Patent, Trademark and Copyright Section of the A.B.A. as well as its Forum Committee on the Entertainment and Sports Industries. In addition to other entertainment-related groups and organizations, he is also a member of the American Arbitration Association's National Panel of Commercial Arbitrators.

Prior to joining Columbia Pictures Television, Hetherington was engaged in private law practice and was a professor of law at Mississippi College School of Law. He started his career with Peer International Corporation/Southern Music Publishing Company, Inc., in New York City, which is one of the largest internationally oriented music publishers in the world.

Hetherington is co-author of the award-winning book *Successful Artist Management,* published in 1979 by Billboard Publications in New York.

Negotiation Strategy for Lawyers

Xavier M. Frascogna, Jr.
and
H. Lee Hetherington

Prentice-Hall, Inc.
Englewood Cliffs, New Jersey

Prentice-Hall International, Inc., *London*
Prentice-Hall of Australia, Pty. Ltd., *Sydney*
Prentice-Hall Canada, Inc., *Toronto*
Prentice-Hall of India Private Ltd., *New Delhi*
Prentice-Hall of Japan, Inc., *Tokyo*
Prentice-Hall of Southeast Asia Pte. Ltd., *Singapore*
Whitehall Books, Ltd., Wellington, *New Zealand*
Editora Prentice-Hall do Brasil Ltda., *Rio de Janeiro*

© 1984 *by*

Xavier M. Frascogna and H. Lee Hetherington

Library of Congress Cataloging in Publication Data

Frascogna, Xavier M.
  Negotiation strategy for lawyers.

  Includes index.
  1. Practice of law—United States. 2. Attorney
and client—United States. 3. Negotiation.
I. Hetherington, H. Lee.   II. Title.
KF300.F7 1984   340'.023'73   84-11776

ISBN 0-13-611237-4

Printed in the United States of America

For Judy, Nan, Marty, and Mike, the ultimate negotiators.

XMF, Jr

To Bav

HLH

Acknowledgments

This book could not have been written without the many contributions of our colleagues, friends, and students, who, over the years, have consciously and unconsciously provided us with ideas, theories, and fresh approaches to this fascinating topic.

A few who have made unusual contributions to this book are: Craig E. Brasfield, Professor Craig R. Callen, E. E. Osadebay, James L. Paul, and Professor Carol C. West.

Special thanks to Alisa Eychaner, Vicki DeAndrea, and Susan Clarey.

Foreword

Negotiation is a game. It's played every day of the year in homes, offices, restaurants, over the phone, and through the mails. Any time two or more people communicate with each other for the purpose of working out problems, resolving conflicts, or changing the status quo, they are negotiating. While we all negotiate, most of us don't depend on the process to earn a living. Lawyers do. Their reputations, self-esteem, and income are significantly affected by their ability to negotiate. With so much riding on this particular skill, it would be only logical to assume that lawyers spend a great deal of their time thinking about ways to improve their overall level of proficiency as negotiators. They don't. There are a lot of reasons why they don't. "I'm too busy." ... "It's not that important." ... "I'm a lawyer, and all lawyers know how to negotiate." The fact is that no lawyer is that busy; nothing could be more important; and lawyers do not have an innate ability to negotiate. Despite this tendency to subordinate negotiation skills in favor of more pressing matters such as reading advance sheets or studying new legislation or regulations, most lawyers are nonetheless adequate negotiators. Because they are intelligent, resourceful, thorough, and more experienced than many nonlawyers they deal with, lawyers generally hold their own when they are called on to conduct a negotiation. There is certainly nothing wrong with being adequate, especially if you're satisfied with this level of proficiency. However, it is our premise that most lawyers aren't satisfied with just getting by. We certainly would not have taken the time to write this book if we didn't truly believe that lawyers want to develop and improve their negotiation skills in the same manner in which they have developed expertise in trial practice or other substantive and procedural areas of the law.

Failure to develop negotiation skills cannot be blamed on the individual attorney. Strange as it may seem, negotiation has always been lost in the shuffle of a lawyer's training. Until recently, few law schools offered courses devoted to the development of negotiation skills. Continuing Legal Education (CLE) programs were more interested in current developments in evidence, tax, corporate law, or what have you—anything but negotiation. There has been a dearth of books and professional articles on the subject as it applies to the practice of law. Law professors, publishers, and others involved in training young lawyers have taken negotiation for granted. Everybody just assumed that negotiation was as natural as riding a bicycle. It's not. Fortunately, all this is changing. Negotiation is suddenly receiving the recognition it deserves. Law schools, bar associations, and legal publishers are focusing their attention on negotiation.

This book is designed to help fill the void that has existed too long. It provides a comprehensive treatment of the various patterns, principles, and techniques that govern negotiation within the context of a law practice. Much of this material is obvious. It is based on common sense and accepted principles of psychology and human behavior. Many experienced attorneys have been using these concepts for years, even though they might not have been consciously aware of what they were doing or why they were succeeding. In addition to easily recognizable principles and techniques, we hope you will encounter some new ideas or fresh applications of old concepts. Regardless of what's old or new, the bottom line is simply this—there are principles of negotiation that work. If you will make the effort to understand and apply these principles systematically, you will get results. Negotiation is a skill, and like any skill, the more you use it, the better you get. This book is intended to serve as a comprehensive tool to help you hone and polish your skills with each new bargaining session you encounter.

From the foregoing material, it's obvious that this is a book for lawyers. However, having a license to practice law is certainly not a prerequisite to receiving tangible benefit from it. It is obviously appropriate for law students who will soon join the ranks of the legal profession. If anything, a law student has the advantage of grasping important principles and techniques that the rest of us have had to learn the hard way through trial and error. Adopting an organized, comprehensive approach to negotiation before representing that first client can give a soon-to-be-lawyer a tremendous professional boost.

The principles and techniques covered in the book can also benefit those who are required to interact and deal with lawyers on a regular basis. Businesspeople, corporate managers, governmental officials, contract administrators, insurance adjusters, purchasing agents, and a hundred other nonlawyer occupational groups can profit from the information covered in this volume. In fact, everyone, regardless of occupation, can benefit from these basic principles that are common to all negotiations.

Regardless of whether you are an experienced attorney, a recent law school graduate, or a person who works in a law-related capacity, you will find yourself spending substantial portions of your time negotiating. This book was written to help you spend that time as productively and efficiently as possible. Any contribution this book might make to your effectiveness will make our time and efforts well worthwhile.

Xavier M. Frascogna, Jr.

H. Lee Hetherington

What This Book Will Do for You

Effective negotiation is essential to the success of any law practice. Despite this basic fact of life, these vital skills have often been lost in the shuffle of a lawyer's training and the day-to-day demands of law practice.

Now, at last, comes the practical help you need to sharpen your negotiating skills for the challenges you face every day of your professional life. *Negotiation Strategy for Lawyers* is a book for lawyers written by lawyers that is uniquely designed to make winning at the negotiating table the norm rather than a hit-or-miss proposition. By following the practical, no-nonsense principles and tactics outlined in this easy-to-read, common-sense guide, you'll find out how to consistently get what you want out of any negotiating session.

Here are just a few of the ways Negotiation Strategy for Lawyers will help you become a better negotiator:

- *It tells how to make the most of your natural advantage as a lawyer and develop an effective negotiating style tailored to your own particular strengths and personality.* You'll discover which negotiating styles work best and how to select an approach to suit each negotiating situation.

- *It gives you a comprehensive blueprint for successful negotiation.* You'll see how to prepare yourself and your client...how to size up the opposition...critical opening moves you should make to seize control of the negotiation from the start. Once you've gained the edge, this guide shows you how to stay in control throughout the negotiation. You'll learn the best time and place to negotiate...how to delay negotiations to buy yourself time...two subtle techniques to keep the negotiation on track...how to pace negotiations to your advantage.

- *It spells out a vast array of tactical negotiating ploys.* You'll see how to set deadlines that will force your opponent to take action...how to use surprise as an effective negotiating tactic...when the best move you can make is no move at all...how to make apparent concessions that are really concession-inducers.

- *It explains how to counterattack your opponent's position.* You'll understand how to employ the "Vanishing Concession" to persuade the opposition to see things your way...how to get stalled negotiations moving again by substituting new players...the "Ultimate Threat" you can use when all ploys fail.

- *It shows you how to deal with the setbacks that are bound to crop up during the course of any negotiation.* You'll learn how to formulate your "Walk Away Position" and when to put it into action...how to make contingency plans...plus more than a dozen actions you can take to help salvage your position when you're really on the ropes.

- *It spells out when and how to handle one of the most delicate aspects of any negotiation: the closing.* You'll find out how to push the deal to a conclusion...three don'ts of closing...and four proven closing techniques for winding up the negotiation.

- *It outlines the best ways to negotiate lawsuit settlements.* You'll learn the essential steps to take to prepare for a lawsuit closing...how to exert maximum pressure on the defendant if you represent the plaintiff...fourteen points to consider when placing a value on your claim...how to find the settlement range...and three fundamentals for successful settlements.

This is just a sample of the kind of valuable help you can expect to find in *Negotiation Strategy for Lawyers*. And perhaps best of all, you'll discover that the tactics and techniques outlined in this guide are explained in the content of general negotiation principles and theory, so that you'll always have a comprehensive frame of reference for approaching any negotiating situation. No matter what your legal specialty—whether it's labor law, corporate acquisitions, personal injury practice, family, general business, or real estate—you'll find that *Negotiation Strategy for Lawyers* will become an essential component of your law library.

Table of Contents

1

Law Practice
Is Negotiation

Law practice is negotiation. Whether you are attempting to conclude an acquisition agreement, trying to settle a personal injury claim, or conferring with a client about pending legal matters, you are negotiating. All of an attorney's legal training and professional expertise is directed toward one objective—solving the client's problems. Negotiation is the primary tool for doing just that. Consequently, those lawyers who can't effectively negotiate can't effectively practice law.

While every lawyer will undoubtedly agree that negotiation is an important skill, few view it as the single most important factor to the overall success of their practice. Be assured that it is. Negotiation is by far the most frequently used device to resolve conflicts and claims. Negotiation is the only process available to form and give order to business relationships. Negotiation is the process that combines legal training and experience with interpersonal skills to achieve tangible results. Negotiation is the action side of a law practice. Consider the following:

- Ninety-five percent of all civil claims are concluded by negotiation, not litigation.
- Of those claims that actually go to trial, only a fraction go to verdict, and of those that do, a substantial portion are settled by negotiation pending appeal.
- Every conceivable type of business relationship is created by negotiation.
- The overwhelming majority of inmates currently serving time in U.S. penal institutions are there because of a negotiated plea bargain.
- Much of our legal system is held together by the central principle of negotiated consensus and agreement.

MAKING THE MOST
OF YOUR NATURAL ADVANTAGE
AS A LAWYER

Lawyers enjoy a decided advantage when it comes to negotiation. While the reasons for this are both real and imagined, the fact remains that lawyers have a head start over the layperson in the give and take of negotiation.

A primary reason for this advantage is based on public perception. The average person untrained in the law views an attorney as being a superior negotiator. This is true even in matters having little or nothing to do with legal issues. After all, giant corporations such as Exxon, CBS, and Xerox turn to legal counsel when it comes to putting together multimillion dollar deals. Professional quarterbacks, rock stars, and network television personalities usually rely on their lawyers rather than themselves when it comes to negotiating big-money contracts. Even the United States government finds it necessary to retain high-powered Wall Street lawyers to help its diplomats deal with complex foreign-policy negotiations such as the Camp David Accords and the Paris Peace Talks. It just stands to reason that lawyers "must" be superior negotiators.

In reality, this perception of superiority isn't always accurate. This isn't to say that a lawyer's advantages as a negotiator are based purely on public misconception. Definitely not. On the average, lawyers are better negotiators than nonlawyers. This is primarily due to experience. Lawyers are simply exposed to more negotiation situations than nonlawyers. This exposure and experience, combined with rigorous educational and licensing requirements, make any attorney a formidable adversary at the bargaining table.

The premise of this book is that most lawyers are generally adequate negotiators and will win their share of negotiations. We believe, however, that most attorneys are not satisfied with just being adequate or with merely winning their share.

POWER NEGOTIATORS

We think most lawyers have the desire and ability to join the elite circle we refer to as "Power Negotiators." In contrast to the average lawyer, Power Negotiators win most of the time. These are the lawyers who have an uncanny knack for overcoming problems, breaking through stalemates, and reaching agreements long after others have given up in frustration. Power Negotiators are nothing more than attorneys who have learned to use the principles of negotiation on a daily basis in their practice. Successful negotiation isn't a skill to these attorneys, it's a habit. The purpose of this book is to help you realize your potential as a Power Negotiator.

THERE'S NOTHING MAGIC ABOUT NEGOTIATION

The first discovery all lawyers have to make is that negotiation is not as mysterious or elusive as they may believe. The lawyers who negotiate multimillion dollar international business agreements don't do it with mirrors or sleight of hand. They employ the basic principles of leverage, timing, knowledge, preparation, and determination to achieve the end result. Instead of searching for magic solutions, they simply rely on the recurrent patterns and principles of negotiation that have withstood the test of time.

Regardless of the complexity or dollar amount involved, these same negotiation principles are equally applicable to the daily problems of all attorneys. To illustrate our point, consider the following excerpts from demand letters seeking to recover damages for a breach of contract. Which do you think would exert more pressure and thus be more likely to yield a more immediate and favorable response by means of a negotiated settlement?

EXCERPT 1

Based on the foregoing, and in order to avoid the expense and inconvenience of litigation, our client would be willing to accept $15,000 in full settlement of this claim. If we do not hear from you within 30 days from the date hereof, we are prepared to pursue our client's legal remedies.

We look forward to hearing from you at your earliest convenience.

Very truly yours,

Frascogna & Hetherington

EXCERPT 2

Based on the foregoing, and in order to avoid the expense and inconvenience of litigation, our client would be willing to accept at this time the sum of $15,000 in full settlement of this claim. If we do not hear from you within 10 days, we will assume that your client has elected not to accept our client's offer of settlement. In such event, we shall withdraw this offer and file an action against you in Federal District Court for the Southern District of New York to recover special and consequential damages in the amount of $55,000 as well as attorney's fees and costs of litigation. We have attached a copy of the complaint as a courtesy to you.

We look forward to hearing from you at your earliest convenience.

Very truly yours,

Frascogna & Hetherington

It's fairly obvious that most attorneys would choose Excerpt 2, but why?

Excerpt 2 utilizes the factors of preparation, credibility, deadline, and uncertainty to enhance the negotiation position of the claimant. These are just some of the techniques that are used time and again by Power Negotiators to achieve immediate results.

THE NEGOTIATING LESSON FROM IRAN

One of the most dramatic negotiations the world has ever witnessed involved the release of the fifty-three American hostages from captivity in Iran. We all recall that on January 20, 1981, after 444 days, they were finally released by virtue of a negotiated settlement directed by the Carter White House. It's no coincidence that the American captives were being sped to the Teheran Airport at the precise moment the presidential oath was being administered to Ronald Reagan, half a world away.

Why? The Iranians were greatly influenced by the power of deadlines. They knew that once the transfer of power to the Reagan administration was completed, the negotiating principals would change. The new administration promised to take a harder line with

Iran. The result: An agreement after fifteen months of deadlock. This deadline factor combined with the uncertainty of a new administration—plus the fact that Iran had already gained maximum publicity value from the hostages and desperately needed money to conduct its war with Iraq—resulted in the agreement that regained the hostages' freedom.

This well-known example stresses the point that there are indeed negotiation principles and concepts that can begin working for you immediately. The key is learning to recognize these concepts and understanding how and why they work. Power Negotiators know that a calculated and planned approach to negotiation based on these principles will always prevail over a lawyer who depends on a bag of random tricks. Our purpose is to help you develop an understanding of these controlling concepts, thereby allowing you to address any problem regardless of the level of bargaining the circumstances may dictate. Such a foundation will allow you to remain unruffled when the tactic that has always worked before fails, or when the other side remains indifferent after you play what you thought was your trump card. This is the difference between an adequate Negotiator and a Power Negotiator.

THERE ARE NO RULES

While there are basic strategies, principles, techniques, and tactics that give form to the negotiation process, there are no rules by which the game is played—except the rules you make, or the ones your adversary makes. To illustrate, consider the following: A resident of New York comes to you claiming he has sustained damages in the amount of $40,000 as the result of the alleged negligence of the defendant, a resident of California. Based on this claim, you advise the plaintiff to file suit in Federal District Court with jurisdiction based on diversity of citizenship. As plaintiff's attorney, you can rely on the Federal Rules of Civil Procedure to provide a framework for the procedural development of your action. Likewise, you know that the rules of evidence will govern admissibility of evidence at trial. All of these rules are uniform and binding on both parties. They provide some assurance that the defendant will file a timely responsive pleading and that each side will have an adequate opportunity to seek relevant facts through discovery. It also helps minimize surprise, delay, or admission of prejudiced statements based on hearsay or undue influence. The primary drawbacks to using the judicial system to resolve this conflict are the expense and length of time involved. This point takes on added significance where the parties have weaknesses or proof problems with their case, or where the amount of money involved would make it uneconomical to proceed to trial.

An alternative to litigation for both parties is to seek a negotiated settlement that potentially could be quicker and less expensive. Assuming this course of action is adopted, the parties, especially the plaintiff, will quickly begin to realize there are no Uniform Rules of Negotiation to ensure fairness, guard against delay, and otherwise guide the negotiation in a predictable, logical manner. The only rules are the ones the parties elect to adopt. There are no others.

For example, if you, as the plaintiff's attorney, write a demand letter to the defendant, there is nothing that requires the defendant to comply with your demand. In fact, the defendant need not respond to the letter. If he does choose to respond, there is no time limit within which he must do so. Assuming the defendant does elect to respond, he controls both the substance and form of that response.

The point to remember is that you as a negotiator are in a position to create, accept, and reject the rules by which a given negotiation will be conducted. Attorneys who recognize and make the most of this fundamental negotiation principle will enjoy a decided advantage over those who allow their opponents to make the rules.

CONSTRAINTS THAT LIMIT
A NEGOTIATOR'S FREEDOM
OF ACTION

While there are no rules governing a negotiation, there are certain constraints that limit a negotiator's freedom of action. Some apply across the board to all negotiators, while others are only applicable to lawyers.

ILLEGAL CONDUCT

A limitation on lawyers and nonlawyers alike are sanctions against illegal conduct, such as fraud, coercion, and conspiracy.

While these provisions by no means ensure honesty and fair dealing, they do set a minimal standard of conduct below which most negotiators are unwilling to venture.

ETHICAL CODES

In addition to legal sanctions, all members of the bar are bound by the American Bar Association's Code of Professional Responsibility. This is an additional check on the conduct of a negotiation by a lawyer who might engage in unethical conduct falling short of a violation of the law.

PROFESSIONAL REPUTATION

A practical constraint on a lawyer's negotiating style is his own professional reputation. While a lawyer is entitled and even required to pursue a client's interests zealously within the bounds of legal and ethical codes, he must take care not to sacrifice his own reputation and credibility by engaging in conduct detrimental not only to the client but to himself as well. Winning at all costs may have the effect of reducing or destroying an attorney's long-term credibility. Representation of a client's interests must be balanced by a sense of propriety and reputation with the practicing bar.

EFFECTIVENESS

An attorney's approach to a negotiation will also be constrained by his ability to achieve workable solutions to a client's long-term as well as short-term problems. For example, assume an attorney is in a position to negotiate a totally one-sided contract in a client's favor by virtue of superior leverage and his understanding of the negotiation process. The client will obviously be pleased in the short run. However, if the contract proves to be so burdensome to the other side so as to be unworkable, the other party may find breach preferable to performance. Should this be the case, the client who was initially satisfied with the negotiated contract will be deprived of his primary objective—a workable agreement. Clients are seldom pleased to find out that they have to litigate what they thought they had already secured through negotiation. Even if the client should win in court, he's still a loser in terms of lost time and expense. The lesson here is to negotiate the most advantageous contract possible for your client that the other side can live with. To go any farther becomes potentially self-defeating.

CONSTRAINTS ARE RARELY UNIFORM

In addition to recognizing the constraints to a negotiation, attorneys should be aware that these constraints will rarely be applied uniformly. For example, while all attorneys are bound by the Code of Professional Responsibility, it should be recognized that there is a wide divergence of acceptable ethical conduct within the Code. The lofty goals of the Code are reflected in the Canons of Ethics, while the minimal standards of acceptable behavior are set forth in the Disciplinary Rules. Technically, opposing attorneys may be in compliance with the provisions of the Code of Professional Responsibility, while the realities and consequences of their behavior are in marked contrast. It is crucial to understand these types of disparities so as not to fall victim to an adversary who may be playing the same game by a different set of rules.

THE CLIENT ONLY UNDERSTANDS
THE BOTTOM LINE

All attorneys know that the ultimate judge of their efforts is the client. The client doesn't understand or fully appreciate the intricacies of the law or your ability to grasp and deal with complex legal problems. The client only understands one thing—results! The negotiation process is the primary vehicle to achieving these bottom-line results.

The purpose of this book is to help you improve your negotiation skills to the point where you win more than just "your share." An understanding of the recurring patterns and principles of negotiation, coupled with an awareness of how to use this knowledge, will pay immediate dividends to you and your clients in terms of bottom-line results.

2

The Power of Leverage

Plaintiffs' lawyers are acutely aware that insurance companies don't settle personal injury claims just to help judges clear crowded dockets or to enable unfortunate accident victims to improve their lot in life. These companies are motivated by one thing—their own self-interest. By paying $10,000 to settle a case, an insurer avoids the uncertainty of an adverse jury verdict that might require it to pay significantly more than the settlement amount. Self-interest is also the principle that controls the creation of business relations. Obviously, television networks don't pay huge sums for the rights to broadcast college and professional football games just to give their commentators and cameramen something to do on Saturday and Sunday afternoons. They are motivated by the leverage of financial opportunity. The networks fully expect to see a return in excess of their investment.

LEVERAGE DERIVES ITS POWER FROM SELF-INTEREST

The power of leverage is grounded on the most basic premise of human existence—self-interest. Except in instances of pure altruism, people are moved to action only when their self-interest is served. Whether self-interest is defined in terms of avoiding potential liability, the prospect of financial gain, or any number of less tangible objectives such as the attainment of good will, improved labor relations, or a heightened degree of prestige, the governing principle remains the same.

13

LEVERAGE IS NEVER STATIC: IT VARIES WITH THE SITUATION

Leverage is by no means a static concept. A lawyer's success in exerting influence will naturally depend on the specific objective sought, the personalities of the people involved, and the circumstances that exist at the time of the negotiation. For example, if you represent a highly paid young wage earner who has been permanently disabled after being struck by a speeding automobile driven by an intoxicated millionaire in plain view of a dozen witnesses, it would be safe to say that you would enjoy a rather strong leverage position. Unfortunately for lawyers, cases involving clear liability or nonliability don't come through their office doors every day. In the more common situation, each side will have strengths and weaknesses. The winner is often determined by who is more resourceful and astute in identifying, assessing, and using the power of leverage.

Regardless of whether you are handling a typical small claims matter or one involving complex, high stakes negotiation, the key to extracting concessions and realizing your objectives is leverage. To illustrate how leverage applies to real-life problems, consider this labor crisis that dominated the national headlines in the summer of 1981.

THE PATCO STRIKE: LEVERAGE ON A NATIONAL SCALE

In August, 1981, President Reagan was confronted with his first major domestic crisis—the air controllers' strike. The controllers sought more money for fewer hours of work in the name of fairness and in the interest of public safety. In the beginning, it appeared that the air controllers union (PATCO) had the upper hand in the confrontation with the government. The threat of thousands of air controllers leaving their jobs across the country was indeed a powerful negotiating lever. The economic concerns of the airline industry and the public's safety fears, not to mention America's commercial and personal dependence on air transport, made PATCO's bargaining position very appealing. In fact, PATCO's position appeared to be invincible. Surely the administration would have to do something to placate the controllers with so much at stake. However, in the end the air controllers either returned to work without any wage increase or were fired. What happened to cause such a reversal of leverage strength resulting in the total failure of the union's demands?

Why PATCO lost its leverage: Despite a strong leverage position, PATCO's leadership miscalculated the strength of its leverage in several ways. The first was an error of perception. The union negotiators on this issue failed to understand the personality of President Reagan. The President had adopted a position supported by personal conviction that no matter how deserving they might be, PATCO's members were threatening to violate a no-strike provision in their contract with the government. Not only was this tactic illegal, but it was a direct assault on one of the President's personal principles, thus requiring him to assume an uncompromising stance. The union simply did not weigh the personality of one of the key players in the drama.

The second major problem revolved around precedent. President Reagan reasoned that if he compromised with PATCO, the die would be cast and a clear message sent to more than two million federal employees who were also suffering from the ravages of inflation. The potential loss for the administration became much greater than simply making a few concessions with a small union. Any concession would be a message to federal employees who had one eye on their paychecks and the other on the evening news. PATCO's threats to the administration's self-interest suddenly took on monumental proportions.

Another explanation for PATCO's loss of leverage was their evaluation of the circumstances surrounding the negotiations with the government. While many Americans were sympathetic to the pleas of the air controllers, the prevailing mood of the country at the time was negative toward wage increases for any particular segment, especially government. This mood had been brought about by the nation's fear of the then-escalating inflation rate coupled with recession and alarm over growing federal budget deficits.

The final straw that broke the union's back related to the use of its leverage position. In the beginning, PATCO evoked sympathy and concern from Americans by demonstrating that their demands were both legitimate and reasonable. However, as the strike deadline neared, their position hardened. It became all or nothing. Suddenly, public sentiment began to shift to the President. The controllers were perceived as being greedy, unreasonable, and totally unwilling to

seek an equitable solution. This was borne out by the fact that the
union had overwhelmingly rejected an apparent settlement that
would have brought them some relief while also averting a strike.
Talks broke off. Instead of attempting to find a way to make progress
on their demands and allow the administration a way to save face, the
union resorted to tough talk and more threats. In response, the
President made a threat of his own that had the support of the
American people; either return to the control towers or lose your job.
Quite simply, the President was prepared to risk the consequences of
having to replace the controllers. As soon as this decision was made,
the controllers lost their primary leverage position. As we all know,
PATCO carried out its threat, and the President carried out his. The
loser: PATCO.

The air controllers' strike is a prime example of the limits of
leverage and the importance of knowing what to do with it once
you've got it.

HOW TO CALCULATE YOUR
LEVERAGE POSITION

The first step to successfully influencing the actions of others
through leverage is to make a realistic assessment of the circumstances surrounding your client's problem. Every negotiation can be
classified in one of three categories based on an analysis of your
alternatives to a negotiated agreement. Naturally, the more alternatives you have, the more leverage you can exert against your
opponent on the other side of the bargaining table. This assessment
will play a major role in the tactics and strategies you select during a
negotiation.

The three basic categories are:

1. The Lost Opportunity Alternative
2. The "Or Else" Alternative
3. The Litigated Alternative

THE LOST OPPORTUNITY ALTERNATIVE

The alternative to agreement in most business negotiations falls
into the "Lost Opportunity" category. It is characterized by parties
seeking to achieve mutual benefits by means of a negotiated agree-

ment, lease, or assignment. A common example is a transaction involving the purchase and sale of real estate. Both the seller and buyer stand to benefit from reaching an agreement provided the terms can be worked out to the mutual satisfaction of the parties. However, if an agreement is not reached, the parties have lost nothing more than the time they have invested in the negotiation and a potential opportunity.

The typical Lost Opportunity negotiation is generally characterized by alternatives on both sides. In an ordinary real estate transaction, there usually will be other potential buyers and sellers. This even split of alternatives begins to shift as the circumstances move away from the norm. For example, suppose the real estate in question happened to be a residence located on Monterey Peninsula's famed Seventeen Mile Drive bordering Pebble Beach Golf Course in California. Further assume that the buyer is a wealthy golfer whose lifetime dream has been to own a home at Pebble Beach. For the buyer, money is certainly a factor, but it is not the overriding consideration. Obviously, if the seller's attorney has access to this information, his leverage position would be greatly strengthened, thereby allowing him to seek a higher selling price and more favorable terms. Alternatively, the buyer's attorney would attempt to project a posture of only passing interest so as not to provide the seller with leverage while attempting to make the most of his own position.

THE "OR ELSE" ALTERNATIVE

This type of negotiation involves a situation in which a solution to the problem could benefit all parties. The alternative to a negotiated solution is an undesirable result in which all parties stand to lose. The classic example of the "Or Else" alternative is collective bargaining between labor and management. A negotiated agreement yields certainty and assures smooth operation for management while providing stable compensation and fringe benefits for labor. The alternative is a strike in which both labor and management would suffer. Where the parties simply can't or won't reach agreement, the ultimate leverage advantage will focus on which party is in a better position to outsuffer the other.

The baseball strike: The unprecedented major league baseball strike of 1981 illustrates this point. After months of talks, the players and owners were at a stalemate over the issue of compensation to be paid by teams signing free agents. The players' primary leverage was the threat of a strike that would shut down the ballparks and deprive the owners of gate receipts and television and radio revenue—a seemingly powerful lever. On the down side, the players were risking their salaries, which were considerable by normal standards. The players reasoned that a strike would hurt the owners more than themselves, thus providing leverage for an ultimate concession on the compensation issue. Their assessment was probably correct, except for one additional factor. The owners had anticipated the players' leverage and responded by purchasing strike insurance, which provided each owner with a payment of $50,000 for each game not played if the players did strike. Additionally, they would not have to meet player payrolls except in the few cases where some superstars had contract clauses requiring a continuation of their salaries in the event of a strike. As the summer wore on, the owners were in no hurry to hammer out an agreement with the players. Two days after the strike insurance expired, a settlement was reached. The relative leverage positions changed. The owners were no longer in a position to outsuffer the players. The result was a new agreement.

THE LITIGATED ALTERNATIVE

This type of negotiation involves claims that, if not settled by negotiation, would be determined by a judge or jury. Usually, in these situations, the gain of one party is tied to the loss of another. The most common illustration of the "Litigated Alternative" is the personal injury claim. The plaintiff seeks a financial settlement with the defendant's insurance company based on alleged legal liability of the defendant. The alternative to a negotiated settlement is to seek a monetary judgment that will be potentially higher than the negotiated conclusion. The best the defendant can hope for is exoneration of liability. Even in total victory, the defendant will usually have to absorb attorney's fees. In this situation, the law supplies the plaintiff with leverage by compelling the defendant to either settle the claim or be exposed to legal liability, provided the plaintiff is able to state a cause of action and sustain the burden of proof. The defendant's leverage revolves around weaknesses in the plaintiff's case. The settlement value will depend on the relevant facts and law, as well as the plaintiff's ability to create uncertainty in the mind of the defendant.

A plaintiff with a marginal claim supported by weak evidence poses no great danger to a well-financed insurance company beyond the nuisance value of the suit. As any defense lawyer will verify, there is a world of difference between filing a lawsuit and winning one.

These illustrations point out the important role alternatives play in determining a lawyer's relative bargaining strength. A clear understanding of your alternatives to an agreement is the first step to creating the leverage power you will need.

THE FOUR LEVERS YOU CAN USE TO MAXIMIZE YOUR BARGAINING POSITION

No two negotiations are ever identical. As mentioned previously, the circumstances, personalities, and bargaining strength of each party will vary with each new situation. Consequently, the specific means employed to influence your opponent's actions will differ depending on these variables. There are, however, four basic levers you can employ in every situation to help maximize your bargaining position. They are:

1. Uncertainty
2. Timing
3. Opportunity
4. Sanction

Practice tip: One or more of these levers will always provide bargaining power no matter how complex or unique the situation. When used appropriately, they can increase your prospects for a successful outcome in any negotiation situation.

UNCERTAINTY

Uncertainty is a powerful negotiating tool that can supply the leverage needed to resolve problems and bring about settlements. Uncertainty uses the element of the unknown to influence the actions and decisions of others.

People tend to worry far more about an anticipated event than the reality of that event once it has taken place. It is this basic fear of the unknown that motivates people to seek as much certainty as possible in their lives. The certain and safe present is always preferred to the uncertain and potentially dangerous future. This is precisely why the lever of uncertainty is such an effective tool in influencing the actions of others. It rests on the premise that people fear taking action.

Uncertainty is built into the legal system: Uncertainty is central to our entire judicial system. The courts represent the last resort to failed negotiations. If you are attempting to negotiate differences, there is at least some element of certainty and control left to the negotiating participants. However, once the matter is referred to a judge or jury, the dispute enters the realm of uncertainty. While the lawyer is still involved in the litigation process, the ultimate decision-making authority has shifted from lawyer and client to judge and jury. Once the dispute reaches trial, lawyers can only predict the outcome. While the lawyer's prediction is certainly an educated one, based on an evaluation of the law, facts, and overall presentation, it is still speculation. The results: anxiety brought on by uncertainty.

Due to the pressures of uncertainty, defendants are moved to settle cases for more than they feel the claim is reasonably worth when faced with maximum exposure that can be ten, twenty, or even thirty times the settlement amount. Alternatively, plaintiffs must weigh the uncertainty of a fixed-sum settlement offer that is substantially below the possible verdict amount. It is precisely this factor of uncertainty that motivates plaintiffs and defendants to settle more than 95 percent of all disputed legal claims.

Uncertainty applies to every negotiation situation: While the Litigated Alternative situation clearly lends itself to the use of uncertainty, this lever is also effective in the "Or Else" and Lost Opportunity Alternative situations. The certainty of settling on a slightly higher purchase price to ensure the acquisition of a prime parcel of real estate may be preferable to the uncertainty of losing the property. The certainty of concluding a collective bargaining agreement at the cost of concessions, even though distasteful, may be better than the uncertainty associated with prolonged negotiation and the possibility of a strike. In every situation, certainty is sought over uncertainty.

Practice tip: For this reason, you should attempt to inject as much uncertainty as possible into a situation without jeopardizing or weakening your position.

Uncertainty is a state of mind: While uncertainty can be an extremely powerful lever, it does have a potential weakness. Uncertainty is nothing more than a state of mind. Once the unknown is explored or experienced, apprehension and anxiety may diminish substantially. If this occurs, the lever of uncertainty can lose its potency. For example, a person who has had past dealings with his opponent is in a much better position to predict his opponent's future actions. Familiarity tends to dilute the strength of uncertainty. This is particularly true where the opposing party or attorney develops predictable patterns that you can anticipate.

Insulate yourself from uncertainty: The lever of uncertainty can be used by either party in a negotiation. Consequently, you should always strive to protect your own positions from the uncertainty that can be exerted by your opponents. The most effective way to insulate yourself from uncertainty is to construct a superior knowledge base. This means checking the veracity of your client's statements as well as those of witnesses and opposing parties. It also means being thorough in your research of the law and facts. The first step in taking the offensive is to ensure that your own position is sound and not vulnerable to the leverage of uncertainty.

TIMING

Knowing when to make an offer, concede a point, or employ a particular strategy is an elusive skill. Those who can consistently make correct timing decisions are rewarded with success at the negotiating table. This is true, even though they may not enjoy a superior bargaining position or may be outmanned in terms of experience and resources.

When should I make my best offer? To illustrate the leverage of timing, consider a common problem facing negotiators. This concerns an answer to the question: At what point should a negotiator make his or her best offer? Some would contend that a fair and generous offer should be made at the outset of a negotiation in order to save time and conclude an agreement in the shortest time possible. While there may be some situations in which this approach might be successful, in most cases such a move would be premature, or ill-advised. The danger lies in the fact that the opposing party is very likely to doubt the sincerity of such an offer. This is especially true if the opponent has prepared for an extended negotiation. An even more dangerous possibility is that the premature offer could be viewed as merely the first of many concessions to come. By allowing time to pass before making the offer, however, the opposing party's expectations of a drawn-out negotiation are met. While it may seem a waste of time, the process of making opening offers, counteroffers, proposals, and concessions is often necessary. This maneuvering may ultimately lead to the same terms originally offered. However, because more time and effort has been invested, your opponent will likely leave the bargaining table convinced he has extracted the best deal under the circumstances. Your opponent's self-esteem remains intact while you have realized your objective.

The role of deadlines: A key to utilizing the leverage of timing is understanding the effect deadlines have on the negotiating process. For instance, why do so many people wait until April 15 to file their tax returns? Why is the short span of time immediately prior to a big event the most hectic? Simply because deadlines motivate people to take action. Successful negotiators take advantage of existing deadlines or create deadlines as a means of exerting leverage. As a deadline nears, pressure mounts and decisions become mandatory. Action is required. Concessions once thought to be out of the question suddenly become workable alternatives. Compromise becomes increasingly more attractive. Nonnegotiable positions are replaced by flexible approaches to solving the problem at hand.

Practice tip: As these examples suggest, timing can take many forms. You should always analyze every negotiation in terms of the leverage of timing. It will always be an element you should consider. Regardless of the circumstances in each case, we urge you to do what's necessary to seize the initiative and turn the clock to your advantage.

OPPORTUNITY

Opportunity is the third major leverage device available to influence the actions of your opponent. The basis of this lever is to use positive reinforcement to induce action. The key to the leverage of opportunity is to identify those points that you can offer to induce a quid pro quo of greater relative value.

Opportunity is anything that will enhance the other party's position or meet his objectives. The least costly application of the "Opportunity Lever" is the apparent concession that in reality is of little or no importance to you, but that is of value to the person to whom it is offered. The level of effectiveness of this tactic will depend on how successful you are in placing value on the opportunity.

The salary negotiation: The typical salary negotiation between an employer and prospective employee is a common example of how the Leverage of Opportunity can be used to your advantage. Let's assume that the employer's objective is to obtain the employee's services at the lowest salary possible. Alternatively, the employee is seeking the most attractive compensation package the employer can afford. Further assume that the employer has recently subscribed to a group insurance plan, the cost of which will be minimally affected by the addition of another employee. Recognizing the prospective employee's desire for fringe benefits such as life and health coverage, the employer offers the insurance plan to the employee in return for a reduction in salary. If the employee agrees, both parties have gained. The opportunity made available to the employee has cost the employer almost nothing in return for a substantial monthly cash savings reflected by the reduced salary. On the other hand, the employee has gained a tangible benefit without having to spend one dollar of his salary for insurance premiums. This is a classic example of win-win negotiation occasioned by the Leverage of Opportunity.

Other applications of the leverage of opportunity may require more substantive concessions. At this point, you must make a judgment as to how much you are willing to give up and how much you stand to receive in return. Only you can make this decision based on complete knowledge of the applicable circumstances and the consequences of your decision.

Practice tip: Never give up something for nothing. In order to maximize the Leverage of Opportunity, you should never give up anything, no matter how seemingly insignificant, without receiving something in return. The degree of return will be dictated by your negotiating objectives. In some instances, the return will be computed in hundreds of thousands of dollars; in others, it may amount to nothing more than an intangible IOU that can be used later. Never lose sight of the fact that what may be insignificant to you may be viewed as something of great value to your opponent.

SANCTION

The "Leverage of Sanction" is the negative counterpart of opportunity. This lever relies on negative reinforcement to compel action. The most common example of the Leverage of Sanction is the threat. If you don't... we'll strike, we'll sue, we'll sell to someone else.... The examples are endless.

The subtle sanction: The Leverage of Sanction can also be exerted by more subtle means that will yield the same results but without the negative overtones that a threat will invariably generate. A recent example involved labor negotiations between the economically plagued United States automobile industry and the United Auto Workers. Against a backdrop of declining sales and record losses during the 1982 recession, General Motors, Ford, and Chrysler told labor that unless they were willing to give up benefits earned in previous bargaining sessions, the auto makers would be forced to lay off workers and close plants to avoid mounting deficits. The approach of management was to portray the possibility of layoffs as a legitimate alternative to dealing with a problem over which it had little control. The car makers were generally perceived by the public as merely communicating a fact of life rather than making a threat. Because the problem was real and the promised sanction credible, the workers responded with unprecedented concessions to avoid losing their jobs.

Making the leverage of sanction work for you: There are several important factors involved in making the Leverage of Sanction work for you. First, you must select a sanction that will be effective in moving the other party. There is nothing worse than threatening a sanction only to be met with the response, "Fine, go right ahead." Second, you must communicate the sanction. As we have seen, communication can range from ultimatums and threats to more subtle statements based on recognition of a mutual problem. In some instances, the communication can take the form of news leaks, planted information, or veiled references in correspondence allowing the other party to gain access to the information indirectly. This approach is often used in diplomatic channels to head off a publicized confrontation. Finally, once the potential sanction is communicated, you must be prepared to carry it out or pay the consequences if the other side regards it as a bluff.

Credibility is absolutely essential when it comes to making effective use of this lever. As mentioned earlier, always remember that the potential for negative fallout is much greater with this lever than any of the others. No one likes to be threatened. When someone pushes you, your natural reaction is to push back. Because of this, your opponent's principles of integrity and self-respect may overrule reason, causing a confrontation that neither side really wants. This is why care and restraint should be exercised in the use of the Leverage of Sanction.

HOW TO COMBINE THE LEVERS TO MAXIMIZE YOUR EFFECTIVENESS

Most negotiations require the utilization of a combination of levers to achieve a client's objectives. It's not uncommon to employ the levers of Uncertainty, Timing, Opportunity, and Sanction within the framework of a single negotiation. The only restriction on the use of leverage is imagination and resourcefulness. The following example illustrates how the four levers can be used in combination to achieve results.

THE MAYOR VERSUS THE TRANSIT WORKERS: THE SUBWAY STRIKE THAT NEVER WAS

Most cities with a bus or subway system have been faced at one time or another with the prospect of a strike. The following scenario has been played out many times. The transit workers' union had been engaged in protracted negotiations with the city administration over the renegotiation of their contract. The union's primary leverage revolved around the threatened sanction of a transit strike that would virtually paralyze the city. The union timed its conduct of the negotiation to ensure that it would go down to the wire. There would be no early solution. The net result of these two factors was the creation of uncertainty in the minds of the public whether the city might be brought to a standstill.

Because the city was experiencing severe financial problems at the time of the negotiation, the administration adopted a hardline stance on any extension of benefits. The city's negotiators decided to fight fire with fire and allow the negotiation to go down to the wire by standing firm and communicating a willingness to accept a strike. The deadline was set for midnight. At 11:30 P.M., word from bargaining headquarters at a downtown hotel was that the talks had collapsed and that a strike was imminent. Many people went to bed prepared for a long walk to work. The next morning, these same commuters were stunned to learn that the strike had been averted. Both the city and union gave ground at the eleventh hour to reach an agreement. This last-minute compromise was produced by the uncertainty created on both sides. As the 12:00 A.M. deadline approached, the city and union decided to soften their positions to take advantage of the opportunity of a predictable and certain agreement to assure the transit workers jobs with liberal benefits in the midst of a troubled economy. On the other side of the table, the city was able to avoid a costly and disruptive strike that would have generated shockwaves far beyond the subway tollbooths.

The subway strike that never was is a dramatic illustration of the power of leverage in action. The same concepts can be applied to the client files on your desk that require a negotiated solution.

3

Personal Negotiating Style: How Leverage Is Used

While the power of leverage is a controlling principle in any negotiation, its true effectiveness will depend on your ability to utilize it. The status quo will always prevail unless and until you take action to transform leverage potential into leverage reality. The more adept you are at recognizing and using leverage, the more successful you will be. This is where the personal component of negotiating style comes into play.

PERSONAL SKILLS VARY: YOUR SUCCESS LEVEL DOESN'T HAVE TO

No two people ever possess precisely the same level of interpersonal skills. Some lawyer-negotiators are simply better with people than others. We all have varying degrees of persuasiveness, resourcefulness, tenacity, and motivation. Despite this fact, there are specific concepts, principles, and patterns that relate to improving your negotiating style. Anyone can improve his basic skills by developing an understanding and appreciation of these factors coupled with a dedicated effort to apply this information to the daily problems associated with his law practice.

WHY IT'S IMPORTANT TO RECOGNIZE YOUR PERSONAL NEGOTIATING STYLE

Your interpersonal strengths and weaknesses as well as your use of leverage, risk taking, aspiration level, ethical considerations, and other components inherent in bargaining all will be reflected in your negotiating style. By understanding what works best for you, you are in a much stronger position to deal effectively with others you will encounter in bargaining situations.

DEVELOPMENT OF YOUR NEGOTIATING STYLE

In order to understand and appreciate fully the various styles we will discuss, it's important to understand how they are developed. A person's negotiating style is generally a reflection of his personality and character. It is molded and shaped from birth. Some of the influences are the result of well-thought-out decisions made at various points in one's professional career. Many others are adopted unknowingly and used unconsciously.

SELF-CONFIDENCE AND YOUR NEGOTIATING STYLE

For purposes of illustration, consider the role self-confidence plays in shaping decisions about how we live our lives. Each of us possesses varying degrees of self-confidence. Self-confidence stems from our ability to triumph over a variety of challenges, problems, and obstacles over a lifetime. Every time we succeed, our confidence is bolstered; every time we fail, our confidence is diminished. With each success, we look for greater challenges and new successes; with each failure, we seek to avoid future challenges for fear of failure. This up-and-down process explains why one's own confidence level is always undergoing change. The older we get, the less dramatic and pronounced the changes. By the time we reach adulthood, much of our confidence level is fixed. Consequently, most of our adult decisions that are affected by self-confidence tend to be consistent and usually predictable.

In the context of a negotiation, the self-confidence of the negotiator will reveal a great deal about how a person is likely to act and react. Utilization of leverage and response to pressure will be affected by this personality characteristic. A person with a relatively low level of self-confidence will likely have lower expectations and will take fewer risks. As a general rule, he will make more concessions and will be more easily intimidated. On the other hand, the self-confident negotiator will expect more, risk more, be less likely to compromise, and be better able to combat superior leverage.

SELF-CONFIDENCE IS ONLY ONE COMPONENT OF YOUR NEGOTIATING STYLE

Self-confidence is only one component of many that combine to shape and mold an individual's personal negotiating style. Other important factors include socioeconomic background, intelligence, education, parental and peer relationships, cultural, geographic and religious background, as well as individual experiences and personal temperament. All of these factors translate into a distinct personality that in turn will determine your specific negotiating style. Your negotiating style remains more or less constant over a lifetime. The older you get, the more difficult it is to change.

RECOGNIZING YOUR WEAKNESSES WILL HELP MAKE YOU A STRONGER NEGOTIATOR

Regardless of how skillful you might be in terms of personal negotiating style, it's only human nature to want to improve. An understanding of your own particular motivations, insecurities, and values is a logical starting point for improvement. While recognition alone won't cure bad habits or eliminate weaknesses, it does force you to face up to them rather than rationalizing shortcomings or placing the blame on more convenient and less personal reasons.

OVERCOMING SHYNESS: AN EXAMPLE OF HOW TO TAKE CHARGE OF YOURSELF

A common problem hindering effective interaction between people is shyness. When this trait is manifested in a negotiation, it can result in a number of potentially negative consequences. As a result of shyness, the negotiator tends to avoid confrontation, makes unnecessary concessions, and fails to exploit negotiating alternatives that require initiating contact with others. This naturally will impede a negotiator's ability to achieve successful settlements and agreements. Once the negotiator is willing to acknowledge his shyness and the fact that it is causing him to be less effective at the bargaining table, he is in a better position to deal with the problem. By making a conscious effort to relate to people rather than avoiding them, one can begin to overcome shyness. Asserting control over a problem is rarely cost-free. The price is usually paid in terms of an increased discomfort level. However, as with anything, the discomfort decreases each time the problem is confronted until a point is reached at which the problem ceases to exist. Over the long run, the negotiator's personal approach and negotiating style is altered for the better as a result of a heightened level of awareness of the factors that help shape his actions.

NO ONE SAID IT WAS EASY

Recognizing a weakness and doing something about it is seldom easy. Many influences and values are so deeply etched on our personalities by a lifetime of reinforcement that it is extremely difficult to deal with them at all. However, there are numerous habits, patterns, and attitudes that contribute to our personal negotiating style that can be improved or altered simply by making the effort to understand them. Regardless of the particular trait you would like to alter or improve, this is the first step. Being honest with yourself and being persistent in dealing with it is the only way you can improve the effectiveness of your personal negotiating style.

THREE NEGOTIATING STYLES: HOW TO SIZE UP YOURSELF AND YOUR OPPPONENT

While no two negotiators are ever precisely the same in terms of approach and style, most adopt one of the three basic negotiating styles. They are:

1. Hardball
2. Softball
3. Give to Get

Practice tip: Each style has recognizable characteristics, advantages, and disadvantages. By understanding these styles, you will be in a much better position to understand yourself as well as your opponent, and to act accordingly.

HARDBALL

Advocates of the "Hardball" negotiating style believe there is no such thing as a marginal victory. You are either a winner or a loser. Because compromise and concession are considered signs of weakness, it is difficult to find a middle ground with a negotiator who wants to play hardball.

The typical Hardball negotiator is usually confrontation oriented. He is hardnosed, aggressive, and competitive. He usually deals from a position of strength and has no qualms about maximizing whatever leverage he has at his disposal. Personal feelings and relationships usually take a back seat to results. Intimidation, threats, and pressure tactics are the hallmarks of a Hardball negotiator's personal style.

A successful Hardball negotiator will usually be prepared and will not make threats he can't back up. Ironically, this credibility also tends to make his bluffs much more believable, allowing him to occasionally win some points on bluster rather than superior leverage.

While Hardball negotiators don't usually win popularity contests, they can be very effective. One advantage of this approach is the ability to exert anxiety and pressure on an opponent, which usually results in a marked increase in concession behavior. This is especially true when the opponent is inexperienced or easily intimidated.

From the client's standpoint, the Hardball negotiator is very effective in portraying strength and dedication to the client's cause. He is especially attractive to someone who wants a hired gun to ensure victory in a high-stakes negotiation. Having a reputation for being tough, thorough, and shrewd will often make opposing lawyers think twice when faced with the prospect of a fight.

Watch out for the drawbacks of Hardball Negotiation: Despite these advantages, there are some obvious drawbacks associated with Hardball negotiation. While it can be effective in eliciting concessions, it also can tend to harden attitudes and polarize positions. This tends to make later compromise much more difficult, if not impossible. High pressure, confrontation-style negotiators also provoke anger and alienation. This can often result in overreaction rather than concession behavior. A negotiator who is threatened or challenged may feel compelled to defend himself and his position at the expense of what might be gained through a negotiated settlement.

As a final long-term drawback, the attorney subscribing to the Hardball Approach should remember that his or her fellow lawyers have keen memories. The Hardball negotiator should be prepared for future encounters with lawyers who might have been the victim of high-pressure tactics in the past. Even if the Hardball approach is used sparingly, it tends to make lasting impressions.

When Hardball works best: Hardball tends to be better suited to negotiations aimed at resolving pending or potential litigation. Generally, it is not the preferred approach for business negotiation, especially when the parties are engaged in a long-term relationship requiring ongoing good faith, trust, and reciprocal dealing. In this situation, a one-sided agreement hammered out by use of superior leverage and hardball tactics may not necessarily be in the long-term best interests of the client. The damage done to personal relationships during the negotiation process combined with onerous terms greatly enhance the prospects for either a breach of contract or less than an enthusiastic effort in performance of contractual obligations. On the other hand, if the parties are involved in a short-term, one-time adversarial business transaction, the Hardball style may prove very effective.

How to keep the Hardball Approach from backfiring: The only effective way to offset the negative aspects of Hardball is to be firm but fair. Objective criteria should be stressed and personalities avoided as much as possible. Threats and ultimatums should not be made lightly. You should always have a reason for using a Hardball tactic. Be aware of the long-term cost that you may be incurring for a short-term result. Once the agreement is concluded, take the initiative to repair any personal damage done in the negotiation. This is absolutely essential if the negative fallout from Hardball Negotiation is to be avoided or minimized.

SOFTBALL

At the other end of the spectrum is the "Softball Approach." It is the antithesis of high-pressure, confrontation-oriented Hardball. It is grounded on the premise that agreements can be reached through cooperation, conciliation, and fair play. This approach puts a premium on personal rapport and friendship. The negotiator employing this style is generally not argumentative by nature or outwardly aggressive. He or she tends to dislike confrontation and will go to some length to avoid it. Apparent sincerity and a low-key personal style are distinguishing characteristics of the person subscribing to this negotiation style.

Softballing does not always spell weakness: At first glance, Softball seems to be nothing more than a euphemism for weakness, appeasement, and problem avoidance. This is not necessarily the case. Depending on the situation and the skill of the negotiator utilizing it, this style can be highly effective. Consider the following example to illustrate this point.

You have been contacted by a former law school classmate and close friend regarding settlement of a contract dispute involving his client and a corporation you represent. After reminiscing about law school days, you finally get around to discussing a settlement. Your friend is very open, admitting that his client is being unreasonable and that he will recommend to him whatever the two of you decide is fair. Based on your relationship with him, you candidly reveal your bottom-line position in an attempt to facilitate a settlement. Upon reflection, you find that you have conceded more than you might have under ordinary circumstances had you been negotiating with a total stranger. In this particular situation, you found yourself bending over backwards because of a personal relationship, possibly to the detriment of your client. Here the Softball Approach was an effective means to bring about a settlement that was both quick and favorable to your mild-mannered law school classmate.

Be aware of the drawbacks to softball: Unfortunately, Softball negotiation is not always as effective as the preceding example suggests. In many instances, it is indeed a euphemism for confrontation avoidance. Many lawyers simply don't like to argue over small points. The truth is that many don't like to argue over big ones either. These negotiators generally have lower aspirations than do their more aggressive counterparts. Merely reaching an agreement, any agreement, often becomes more important than the terms embodied in the agreement. While personal relations are maintained and strengthened by this approach, effectiveness often suffers. This is especially true when the lawyer sitting across the table is not willing to make concessions and reveal information in order to preserve and promote a personal relationship. When this is the case, the negotiator using the Softball philosophy will find himself striking out.

GIVE-TO-GET: THE MIDDLE GROUND

The "Give-go-Get" Approach represents the middle ground between the previous two extremes. It rests on the premise that few negotiators will have sufficient leverage and personal skill to achieve satisfactory results using the Hardball approach, and that Softball is rarely effective on a consistent basis. As a result, your aspirations must, by necessity, be adjusted to achieving as many realistic objectives as possible while allowing the other party to realize his objectives to the extent the aspirations of the parties are not inconsistent or mutually exclusive. The remaining objectives that do conflict can be resolved by compromise. The Give-to-Get approach rests on the pragmatic recognition that a shared victory through agreement is generally preferable to a total victory by other, more expensive and time-consuming means. Only when the benefits of an agreement are outweighed by an alternative method of dealing with a specific problem should you forsake the negotiated settlement.

Be creative but firm: The Give-to-Get philosophy encourages a creative approach to negotiation based on communication and satisfaction of mutual concerns and objectives. Since this is basically a cooperative approach, the negotiator's personal style, by necessity, is usually friendly but firm. The negotiator utilizing this approach must constantly ask himself, "What can I concede to my opponent that will result in the least concession and the greatest gain?" If most of each negotiator's objectives can be realized at a relatively low cost in terms of concessions, the remaining compromise will seem much more palatable. This approach allows both parties the psychological benefit of feeling like a winner when the final results are tabulated.

This is not to suggest that the middle-ground Give-to-Get approach consists only of compromise between two positions. There are often situations in which the negotiators can achieve their respective goals by finding mutually agreeable solutions to common problems. This was illustrated by the salary negotiation in Chapter

Two. The employee gave up added taxable income in favor of securing increased insurance benefits at no additional cost to him. The employer, on the other hand, maximized use of his insurance plan while saving an additional out-of-pocket expense in the form of paying a higher annual salary to the employee. Here, the real essence of giving to get revolved around each side giving up the idea that one position must prevail over another—i.e., employee's gain must be tied to employer's loss in favor of a mutual process that yields a solution without regard to position. When it is possible to use this tack, you should. Unfortunately, in the real world of negotiation, creativeness will not overcome the reality that there will be situations in which one party's gain will invariably be tied to another's loss. At this point, the Give-to-Get approach takes on more characteristics of pure compromise and less of joint problem solving.

Advantages and disadvantages of Giving to Get: Regardless of what form the Give-to-Get approach takes, a major advantage of this approach is that it facilitates more workable, long-term solutions to problems while preserving personal relationships. It does, however, require you to rethink your objectives in less selfish terms and exert greater patience and creativity to make it work. Unfortunately, not all lawyers are willing to make such an adjustment. It's tough to find common ground or help the other guy solve his problems when all he wants to do is push you into a corner and keep you there.

WHICH STYLE IS BEST?

If you were asked to choose the best negotiating style from the four choices set forth below, which would you select?

    (a) Hardball
    (b) Softball
    (c) Give to Get
    (d) None of the above

Before you answer, you should know that most negotiation theorists clearly favor (c). However, the inescapable answer for a pragmatic lawyer who deals in bottom-line results is (d). Here's why:

LACK OF CONTROL
OVER UNCONSCIOUS FACTORS

First of all, in light of all the unconscious factors that influence the development of our personalities, it is unrealistic to suggest that a negotiator can select a new style simply by electing to do so. Such a change would require a complete personality transformation. This is further complicated by the fact that every negotiator's personal style is a blend of varying degrees of each of the three models discussed, with one usually being predominant. From a practical standpoint, it would be impossible merely to choose one over the others.

FLEXIBILITY: THE KEY TO
AN EFFECTIVE OFFENSE

The effective negotiator armed with knowledge and understanding of these three dominant personal styles is in the enviable position of being able to use aspects of each that correspond to the personalities, circumstances, and objectives involved in a given negotiation. Staying flexible also helps guard against the silent enemy of predictability. An emphatic demand or show of anger by a negotiator who characteristically is amiable and noncombative will likely make a significant impression on a person not accustomed to this behavior. Emphasizing joint problem solving, the Give-to-Get approach will be an effective tool in the hands of a Hardball negotiator who has little leverage available to him in a particular negotiation.

FLEXIBILITY: THE KEY TO
AN EFFECTIVE DEFENSE

From a defensive standpoint, flexibility can likewise be an effective and sometimes decisive weapon. As mentioned earlier, it is difficult to make Softball or even Give-to-Get work when confronted with an aggressive Hardball-style negotiator armed with superior leverage. By being aware of each of the negotiating styles, the normally congenial lawyer can adjust his style to offset an opponent's tactics without falling into many of the traps or pitfalls associated with each. For instance, suppose an aggressive, litigation-oriented lawyer tries to exploit your position with a threat, knowing it is not your style to make threats in return. Assume he also knows that his position is tenuous, but feels he can bluff his way through. The lawyer who understands the Hardball style and is aware of his opponent's relative lack of leverage to back up his threat can devastate the opposition with an unexpected threat of his own coupled with a subtle hint that he is fully aware of his opponent's bluff tactics. Here, this uncharacteristic adjustment in tactics coupled with superior knowledge will be enough to turn the tables against a blustering opponent.

THE CRYSTAL BALL FACTOR: READING THE OPPOSITION

One of the most useful aspects stemming from an understanding of negotiating styles is its predictability value. As we have seen, each negotiating style has its own particular characteristics that are suprisingly consistent. The negotiator who can pinpoint his opponent's style is in a much stronger position to anticipate the tactical moves that will be employed against him. By taking the mystery out of your opponent, you are able to neutralize and offset his moves, while also reducing the anxiety and uncertainty he seeks to create in you.

OFFSETTING A HARDBALLER

For instance, if you recognize your opponent as a Hardball Negotiator, you know that chances for an agreement are highly remote until a deadline presents itself or a sanction is carried out. If the specific problem involves potential litigation, you can count on your opponent to file suit before a settlement is possible. This knowledge frees you from the anxiety and uncertainty created by your opponent's threat to file a law suit absent a concession on your part. In effect, you have neutralized his leverage on this particular point by not falling victim to the anxiety your opponent sought to induce. At the same time, you have gained the advantage of spending more time in preparation for your defense of the suit rather than wasting your time trying to forestall it.

WHEN GIVE-TO-GET IS BEST

On the other hand, if your opponent shows signs of using the Give-to-Get approach, you know you can spend your time effectively trying to understand his needs and objectives. This would probably be a waste of time if your opponent elected to play Hardball and largely unnecessary if his game was Softball.

YOUR KNOWLEDGE OF NEGOTIATING STYLES IS A KEY TO BOTTOM-LINE SUCCESS

In short, understanding the characteristics of the three predominant negotiating styles can be a valuable asset in constructing your own negotiating blueprint as well as reading your opponent and responding to his plan of attack. The charts that follow provide a quick reference for doing just this. This analysis should be an automatic part of your preparation for any negotiating encounter.

Practice tip: Be aware of the characteristics of the three predominant negotiating styles—then try to use aspects of each style when the opportunity to do so presents itself.

HARDBALL	
ADVANTAGES	DISADVANTAGES
1. Tends to produce one-sided agreements that are advantageous if performed. 2. Elicits more concessions from opponent. 3. Exerts a higher degree of anxiety and pressure on opponent. 4. Substantiates deadline demand. 5. Establishes hardnosed image and reputation. 6. Displays strength to client. 7. Extreme demands can result in higher settlements and attainment of objectives.	1. One-sided agreements are often breached or not enthusiastically performed by parties who have little incentive to live up to the bargain. 2. Causes anger and alienation. 3. Polarizes positions. 4. Tends to cause overreaction. 5. Tends to impair and sometimes destroy personal relationships. 6. Damages future relations with attorneys or parties you will negotiate with again. 7. Hardnosed image and reputation difficult to shed.

SOFTBALL	
ADVANTAGES	DISADVANTAGES
1. Avoids confrontation. 2. Uses emotional aspect to persuade. 3. Can pivot for change of tactics. 4. Maintains and strengthens personal relations. 5. Decisions made without the influence of anger or overreaction.	1. Too many concessions. 2. Deadline threats can become meaningless. 3. Establishes a weak negotiating image with fellow attorneys. 4. Displays an image of weakness to the client. 5. Can result in poor settlements and failure to achieve client objectives.

GIVE TO GET	
ADVANTAGES	DISADVANTAGES
1. Tends to produce mutually acceptable agreement. 2. Encourages concessions from all parties. 3. Displays the reasonable man image. 4. Tends to build personal relationships between negotiators. 5. Forces the negotiator to control anger.	1. Sacrifices total victory for joint solution. 2. Difficult to use if other side refuses to cooperate. 3. Difficult to employ when dealing from a position of weakness or a defensive posture. 4. Difficult to use when there is personal dislike or mistrust of the opponent. 5. Requires more time.

CHARACTERISTICS OF THE THREE NEGOTIATING STYLES		
HARDBALL	SOFTBALL	GIVE TO GET
1. Aggressive nature 2. Angers easily 3. Likes to intimidate 4. Abrupt and short 5. Limited communication 6. In a hurry 7. Negotiation by ultimatum 8. Rejects suggestions 9. No concession until the deadline	1. Friendly 2. Never angers 3. Too much communication 4. Never threatens 5. Readily accepts suggestions 6. Concessions freely given	1. Friendly but firm 2. Controls anger 3. Open-minded 4. Open communication 5. Likes to bargain 6. Adopts a creative approach 7. Analyzes suggestions

4

Preparation:
The Essential
Ingredient for Success

Good negotiators are prepared. They know where they are going as well as when and how. Superior preparation can often spell the difference between winning and losing, especially in hard-fought, complicated bargaining contests. Even in the simplest matters, preparation is the element that allows you to weave relevant information and applicable negotiating principles into a winning result.

Unfortunately, preparation takes time, a commodity that is at a premium in any busy law office. The alternative to spending the necessary time to prepare is generally reflected by a losing performance at the bargaining table.

Practice tip: When it comes to preparation, there is only one choice for successful negotiators. Do it. That means taking the necessary time to ensure that your assumptions and information are accurate, thorough, and in sufficient detail to allow you to take charge of a negotiation. This is the only way to avoid being dragged along by circumstances, the opposing attorney, or both.

When it comes to preparation, too many lawyers reinvent the wheel every time they are confronted with a new negotiating problem. Others never get around to inventing the wheel in the first place. Both of these preparation problems are unnecessary. This chapter is devoted to helping you streamline your preparation and make the most of the time you have.

TAKING A LONG-RANGE VIEW OF PREPARATION WILL PAY DIVIDENDS

Many effectiveness problems relate to a narrow view that some lawyers have of preparation. There is a great deal more to preparation than just gathering facts about a particular personal injury claim or formulating a list of demands in a property settlement negotiation. Besides these essential short-term considerations, there are very important long-range aspects to preparation that relate to image, interpersonal skills, goal formation, and strategic planning that should be carefully considered and addressed. Many of these are extremely powerful, although often subtle, making it easy to over-look, minimize, or dismiss their importance. Successful negotiators recognize their importance and emphasize the role they play in their overall approach to negotiation. If you aren't dealing with them, now is a good time to start. Many of the elements we will discuss are long-term in nature and aren't usually considered under the topic of preparation—but in a strategic sense, they are. Dealing effectively with each of them will pay enormous long-term dividends.

This chapter is concerned with both long- and short-term aspects of preparation. A balanced concept of preparation can increase your effectiveness while decreasing the hours necessary to prepare adequately for a winning negotiation.

THE ROLE PEOPLE SKILLS PLAY IN SUCCESSFUL NEGOTIATION

For some reason, lawyers have always been led to believe that just because they hold a license to practice law they are also expert interviewers, counsellors, and negotiators. This is simply not true. In actuality, few attorneys actually try to develop a comprehensive approach to dealing with people. There is often little or no thought given to why one deals with people in a certain way and if there might be a more efficient way of achieving the same results. This haphazard approach is reflected by settlements that are less than satisfactory, contracts with too many concessions, and clients who never come back. Unfortunately, in an overwhelming number of instances this failure to operate at optimum effectiveness is due to lack of development of interpersonal skills. Fortunately, however, once these skills are learned, they become automatic. The positive effects they engender enure to your benefit throughout your professional life. These factors deal primarily with interaction and communication skills.

Practice tip: A conscious effort to develop these skills should be part of your long-range view of preparation.

POWER OF THE FIRST IMPRESSION

We all know from experience the power that first impressions play in our dealings with others. The first impression warrants special significance whenever lawyers become involved. Clients and other lawyers often carry preconceived notions about a particular attorney into the first encounter with that person. Preliminary impressions will either strengthen one's positive perceptions about the lawyer or will raise and reinforce doubts about him. Needless to say, a favorable first impression will get a negotiation off on the right track and keep it there.

Appearance: Before you say a word, your appearance will generate signals to a client or opposing attorney. As common sense and experience demonstrate, a smiling and energetic facial appearance will go a long way in projecting a favorable image. Lawyers who have pleasant personalities and maintain a positive mental attitude just naturally attract clients and project positive impressions to other lawyers. While this may seem elementary, take time to observe your initial reaction to others and your basis for those reactions. You are likely to be surprised by the intensity of your impressions, both positive and negative. Keep in mind that this process is going on constantly with others you encounter—the only difference is that you are the one they're sizing up.

Dress: Dress conservatively and tailor your wardrobe to the occasion. Continuity of image is best served for men by the dark blue or gray suit, solid white or blue dress shirt with a button-down collar, conservative regimental tie, and dark shoes and belt. For women, a no-nonsense blue or gray suit with a white silk blouse is always appropriate. Interestingly enough, there are some wardrobe authorities who draw distinctions between when the lawyer should wear a blue or gray suit and when an Ivy League or regimental tie should be worn. These clothing experts make a good case for varying the color of clothing to make different psychological impressions on juries.

POWER OF PERSONAL PERCEPTIONS

An important part of developing people skills is having the ability to recognize and react to the perceptions and needs of clients, adversaries, and opposing attorneys. This is analogous to a quarterback reading the opposing team's defense and then calling his next play accordingly. To be successful, you must be able to read other people to determine how you are being perceived. Once you understand how the client or opposing attorney views you, you can act accordingly to achieve optimum results.

As mentioned earlier, every lawyer, judge, or client brings with him certain preconceived impressions about lawyers in general and you in particular. In most cases, these perceptions will be a jumble of feelings, emotions, and expectations, some of which will be valid while others will belong strictly to the realm of fiction. Regardless of the validity of these preconceived perceptions, you have no choice except to deal with them. The more you are able to measure up and reinforce positive perceptions while dispelling negative ones, the more satisfactorily a given transaction will go. Once the opposing lawyer makes a determination that you are competent and honest, he will naturally drop a certain degree of guarded reserve. This makes any working relationship much easier and more productive. This is why it is important to survey the opposing attorney's perceptions about you and then respond with the right signals. Unfortunately, too many lawyers miss this point altogether. They flounder through a negotiation wondering why a rapport never materialized. There is usually a reason. It's much better to find out what that reason is before irreparable damage is done to your prospects for a successful outcome to the negotiation.

POWER OF NATURAL ADVANTAGE

Because of your status as a lawyer, you enjoy certain natural advantages when it comes to dealing with people on a professional basis, especially clients. If you are to negotiate effectively on behalf of a client, it is essential that your relationship with the client be based on confidence, trust, and open communication. Your natural advantage can help create such a relationship.

One advantage you enjoy as a lawyer is that your clients voluntarily seek out your advice. This means that your client has made an independent decision that he has a problem and needs professional help. Under these circumstances, the client is much more likely to tell you what's on his mind and to listen to what you have to say.

Practice tip: Your words, actions, and demeanor should be calculated to reinforce the fact that the client has made the right decision in coming to you. You should also reassure the client that you are interested in what he has to say and encourage him to confide in you regarding all relevant details of the problem. This is a technique that can result in instant positive rapport while ensuring that you are getting a complete picture of the client's particular situation.

Take charge of the initial meeting: Nonlawyers generally regard lawyers as authority figures who possess superior intelligence, knowledge, and experience. Additionally, most attorneys are perceived as being organized and accustomed to taking control of problem situations. For these reasons, clients are much more apt to let you set the pace. This means you have a head start in controlling the relationship. It's important that you take advantage of this opportunity by taking charge of the initial meeting. Don't wait for the client to set the tone of the relationship. If you do, you most likely will appear to be weak and indecisive.

Be objective: Because you are representing the interests of others, you have the advantage of detached objectivity that generally is not enjoyed by your client. If you allow yourself to become too emotionally involved in your client's problem, you run the danger of losing this natural advantage. While it's important that you be committed to your client's cause, don't become emotionally caught up with your client's problem to the extent that you do not look at the weaknesses of his position, or fail to verify the accuracy of your client's story.

Be skeptical: Lawyers are trained to be skeptics. You should never accept everything someone tells you at face value. It is your job to satisfy yourself as to the accuracy and validity of a given statement or proposition. This skepticism is a decided advantage when representing the overly optimistic business client who wants to dwell on the positive while ignoring the pitfalls of a deal or an intimidated civil or criminal defendant who is convinced that only the worst will come to pass.

There are situations when you can become too devoted to your client's cause. When this happens, there is a tendency to make the client's problems your own. The case becomes a personal crusade, causing the lawyer to lose sight of the client's concerns, needs, and objectives. Beating the other lawyer becomes the sole objective and criterion for success. Inflexibility and reticence may replace calculated objectivity, resulting in decisions based on emotion rather than reason. You should take great care to avoid these all too human tendencies.

POWER OF EFFECTIVE COMMUNICATION

Regardless of whether you are trying to advise a client, solicit information from a witness, or persuade another attorney to accept a negotiation point, a key to your level of effectiveness is your ability to communicate.

Illustrations of faulty communication are abundant. One notable example revolves around a foreign marketing campaign conducted several years ago by a major U.S. auto manufacturer. The automaker sought to create a demand for its midsize Nova automobile in several Latin American countries. The Nova had achieved a high degree of popularity in the United States. In light of this success, company executives reasoned that it could do equally well in foreign markets. The Nova was introduced to Spanish-speaking consumers who overwhelmingly rejected the product. The reason for the failure? Very simple: In Spanish the phrase "no va" means "no go." A simple breakdown in communication had a direct and substantial negative impact on bottom-line results. The same danger is ever-present in the sphere of legal negotiation.

EFFECTIVE COMMUNICATION IS SIMPLY
A MATTER OF PREPARATION

Effective communication, whether oral or written, requires a great deal of care, preparation, and practice. While the entire process of effective communication could fill a separate volume, the following principles should serve as a foundation for your communication skills.

Be precise: We all know the dangers of a vague or ambiguous clause in a contract or will. The true intent of the parties is obscured or blurred because of imprecise expression. This same danger exists within the context of a negotiation. The value of a solution to a negotiation problem is only as good as your ability to express it and have it understood. This is why precision in word selection, and care in how those words are presented, is vitally important.

Keep it simple: Verbosity seems to be an occupational hazard for lawyers. It shouldn't be. You can avoid this stumbling block by being simple, direct, and to the point. Too many lawyers have a deadly fear of periods and two-syllable words, favoring instead semicolons and fifty-cent words.

Practice tip: This problem is easily corrected if you will remember the following axiom: After you've said what you have to say as succinctly as you know how, stop.

Be an active listener: How many times have you been introduced to someone only to find that you don't know their name five minutes later? Why does this happen? Possibly because you were introduced to Yanokan Czintrolansk or Machenshu D. Abundanutitus, but more probably because you failed to listen actively to the other person's name when the formal introduction was made. Real listening requires disciplined concentration. This can prove to be a considerable challenge, especially when the person you are listening to is the personification of rambling imprecision and chronic verbosity. Any lawyer knows from experience that a number of clients and too many lawyers tend to fit this description. This is why it is doubly important to develop good listening habits that will allow you to ferret out relevant information and ask probing questions designed to cut through the verbiage and get to the problem. Sustained active listening is by no means easy, but it is essential to your success as a negotiator.

Watch your interruptions: One final key to active listening is being conscious of interruptions. There is a natural tendency to interject a comment or idea without letting the person who is talking complete his statement. As a result, we spend more time preparing our own rejoinders than we do listening to what the person on the other side of the conversation has to say. As a result, you are not hearing a portion of the message. This opens the door to misunderstandings rather than to solutions.

Practice tip: Once you adopt and practice these basic principles of human interplay and communication, they will become automatic. The advantages to be gained will serve you for a lifetime.

SHORT-TERM PREPARATION: GETTING READY TO NEGOTIATE

The preceding material dealt with factors that tend to have an indirect, long-term effect on all negotiations. Often these factors are scarcely noticed and tend to work in extremely subtle ways. In contrast, the second category of preparation will have a direct impact on the negotiating process. This section is primarily concerned with the formulation of realistic goals as well as the selection of the proper strategy and tactics to achieve the desired results.

FIND OUT WHAT YOUR CLIENT WANTS FROM A NEGOTIATION

The first area of inquiry all negotiators must address deals with finding out exactly what the client wants from a negotiation. Unfortunately, determining the client's true wishes can often be difficult and in some cases a never-ending process. Nonetheless, the heart of any negotiation centers around getting the client what he wants. An essential part of your preparation is to find out what that is.

CATEGORIZE YOUR CLIENT'S OBJECTIVES

The client's goals can be divided into three types. "Deal Points" are those the client absolutely must have in order to realize his primary objective. "Secondary Points" involve goals that are important but not necessarily vital to the client. "Trade Points" are lower-priority goals the client would like to achieve, but which will not play a substantial role in the overall success or failure of the final agreement. From a tactical standpoint, trade points are extremely important to a skillful negotiator. While they are of little value to the client, they can often be converted into valuable secondary or deal points in the mind of an opponent, thus allowing the negotiator to induce a swap for something of greater value from the opponent. We will further discuss these and other tactical considerations in the chapters that follow.

TWO KEY QUESTIONS THAT WILL REVEAL
YOUR CLIENT'S REAL OBJECTIVES

During the initial client interview, you should give your client the opportunity to tell his complete story before you start addressing specific issues through questioning. Once all the relevant facts have been elicited, you should focus on your client's specific goals. This information can be obtained by asking two questions during the interview:

1. If you could have everything you want in this negotiation, what would you desire in the final agreement?
2. If everything goes against us in this negotiation, what would be the very least you would accept to conclude an agreement?

DEAL POINTS	1. _____
	2. _____
SECONDARY POINTS	1. _____
	2. _____
TRADE POINTS	1. _____
	2. _____
	3. _____

HOW TO PREPARE
YOUR NEGOTIATING STRATEGY

The next step in the preparation process is selection of the particular strategy that will be followed throughout the negotiation. Strategy decisions should answer the question, "How will I achieve my client's objectives?" For instance, in a personal injury case some lawyers adopt a strategy of filing the lawsuit before commencing negotiations. Others employ just the opposite approach by immediately entering into negotiations and using the threat of a lawsuit as leverage throughout the discussions. Strategy is the direction in which one moves toward one's goal. The actual mechanics of taking specific action will be embodied in the tactics you employ to reach your bargaining objectives.

Strategy will be determined by a number of factors, including the negotiating style of both you and your adversary, specific facts and circumstances, and relative leverage positions. All of these factors should be analyzed and catalogued in a manner that will give you instant access to them. Essential facts and leverage positions should be simplified and put in outline form. This visual overview will be a great aid when developing an overall strategy and specific tactics.

Consider asking variations of these key questions in order to determine the client's real goals. Repetition is the key to gaining this important information. The client's response to these questions will provide you with a negotiating target. If your client's goals are unrealistic, you can take the necessary action to reduce his expectation level. Reference to unfavorable statutes, case law, verdict expectancy statistics, and your overall judgment as to your client's chances for success can help in adjusting your client's goals to a more realistic level. If this is necessary, it is especially important to do it at the outset of the lawyer-client relationship, before your client develops an unrealistic, rigid, and uncompromising mindset. On the other hand, if your client has adopted a low expectation level, you may want to reinforce this position in order to insulate him from possible disappointment. If it turns out that the final result is in excess of your client's expectations, all the better.

After a thorough interview and analysis of your client's response to the key questions mentioned above, the three categories of goals will emerge. You can then proceed to the next step of Goal Formulation.

GOAL FORMULATION

Once you have identified the client's goals, you are then in a position to organize them in the order of importance.

Strategy is important in negotiation because it gives shape and direction to the isolated moves you will make. Strategic planning facilitates tactical decision making designed to move you to your final objective. On the other hand, negotiating without strategy usually results in random selection of tactics that bring hit-and-miss results. For instance, in the personal injury example mentioned above, if the lawyer had adopted a strategy of withholding the filing of a lawsuit as long as negotiations were ongoing, he would not threaten to file suit at every impasse during the negotiation. Instead, the subtle threat of suit would be interwoven in the entire pattern of the negotiation. On the other hand, lawyers adopting the sue now, talk later approach would be in a better position to use the threat of suit in the initial meeting with the opposition.

HOW TO SIZE UP THE OPPOSING PARTY

To a great extent strategy and tactics will be determined by the objectives of the opposing party. You should accumulate sufficient information in your opening moves to identify or at least shed light on your opponent's goals. This information then should be charted as follows:

OPPONENT'S DEAL POINTS	1. _____ 2. _____
OPPONENT'S SECONDARY POINTS	1. _____ 2. _____ 3. _____
OPPONENT'S TRADE POINTS	1. _____ 2. _____ 3. _____ 4. _____

After an analysis of your opponent's goals has been completed, you should compare the objectives of all the parties in the negotiation and proceed with your strategy decisions.

CLIENT'S DEAL POINTS	OPPONENT'S DEAL POINTS
SECONDARY POINTS	SECONDARY POINTS
TRADE POINTS	TRADE POINTS

A WORD OF CAUTION: STAY FLEXIBLE BECAUSE GOALS CHANGE

We must issue a word of caution—goals can change and often do. Just because you accurately perceive your opponent's objectives today does not necessarily mean his objectives will remain constant over the course of the negotiation. The longer a negotiation is drawn out, the greater the likelihood that one of the parties will change his objectives. This is why one of the most successful tactics used by defense lawyers is delay. Protracting a negotiation frequently causes adjustment in one of the parties' expectation levels. Even though anyone is susceptible to altering their objectives, completing the goal analysis at the outset will, at the very least, provide you with the parameters of the negotiation. Identifying the goals of all the parties is analogous to drawing the boundaries of an athletic playing field before the game. Knowing where the game will be played is always preferable to looking for the stadium and never finding it.

MAKING THE PLAN WORK:
LAWYER SHARP VERSUS THE RECORD COMPANY

Once you have completed the planning phase, the process enters the realm of pure negotiation. You will attempt to maneuver your opponent toward an agreement that will fulfill your client's objectives.

To illustrate the entire process of goal formulation and the other aspects of prenegotiation organization, let us consider the following example.

Lawyer Sharp has been retained by a local rock band to negotiate a recording contract with a major record label. From his initial interview with the band, he learns that the prospect of a local rock band being offered a contract with a major record label is a one-in-a-thousand chance. Because of this reality, the band is more concerned about blowing the deal than pressing the record company on the fine points of the agreement. On the other hand, Lawyer Sharp knows from experience that the excitement of the moment will diminish once the agreement is finalized and the realities of doing business with the record company begin. He knows that in later years the band will look to him and ask why the record company was given certain powers in the agreement and why he can't "get them out of the deal" if the situation sours. So with this background in focus, Lawyer Sharp constructs the following chart:

CLIENT'S DEAL POINTS	1. Consummate a deal with the major record company.
SECONDARY POINTS	1. Amount of royalty on record sales to be paid band.
	2. Amount of advance money paid to band.
	3. Length of agreement.
	4. Number of options given record company.
	5. Amount of tour support allocated to band by company.
	6. Exclusivity and scope of the recording agreement.
TRADE POINTS	1. Previously recorded product of the band.
	2. Artist warranties.
	3. Jurisdiction/venue of agreement.

The record company has already forwarded a copy of its standard recording artist agreement to the band for their review. The band is of the opinion that the agreement is fine. The members are ready to sign, but they want Lawyer Sharp to advise them about certain provisions of the agreement. Not surprised, Lawyer Sharp explains that the agreement doesn't give the band exactly what they expected and suggests that he be allowed to negotiate with the record company on their behalf. They agree, but caution Lawyer Sharp, no matter what, don't blow the deal!

The first step Lawyer Sharp takes is to engage in several telephone conversations with the record company's general counsel regarding some highly technical provisions of the agreement. From these conversations, he is able to gain valuable information about the technical aspects of the agreement as well as learn about company policy as it relates to its recording contracts. He discovers through these conversations what points are of primary importance to the record company and, just as important, why the record company has certain concerns about specific points of the agreement. Based on this information, he is able to formulate what he believes are the record company's goals in this particular negotiation.

OPPONENT'S DEAL POINTS	1. Consummate the deal with the band on favorable terms.
SECONDARY POINTS	1. Exclusivity and scope of this agreement.
	2. Length of the agreement (including options).
	3. Previously recorded product.
	4. Advance money to be paid band.
	5. Royalty to be paid band.
	6. Jurisdiction/venue.
TRADE POINTS	1. Tour support.
	2. Artist warranties.

Lawyer Sharp's goal analysis provides him with an overview of the relevant factors that will influence the negotiation. Based on his assessment of these factors, he concludes that this situation will dictate a strategy of extreme cooperation with the record company. His relative lack of leverage will require him to use soft pressure to gain concessions for his clients. The adoption of the softball approach in this situation eliminates many aggressive tactics that might be appropriate if a tougher strategy could be employed. However, under present circumstances, Lawyer Sharp believes he has made a well-thought-out decision based on the facts and the goals of his clients. From this point, it becomes a matter of pure negotiation with Lawyer Sharp selecting the proper tactics to deliver the desired result.

PREPARATION IS WORTH THE EFFORT

As the preceding material and examples illustrate, the key to organizing for a negotiation is preparation. It's not glamorous, it takes time, and it is often frustrating. It's also the only method yet devised that brings order to the seemingly unending stream of facts, impressions, perceptions, and tactics that go into defining the bottom line. Taking the time to prepare is worth the effort—once you get to the bargaining table, you'll be glad you did.

5

Opening Moves:
How to Seize
Control of
the Negotiation

You are an attorney representing a major manufacturing concern. The president of the company authorizes you to begin secret negotiations to acquire controlling interest in a competitor corporation. What is your opening move?

Your law firm specializes in insurance defense. You receive word that a $2 million personal injury suit has been filed against your client's insured stemming from a multiple-fatality construction accident. What is your opening move?

A well-known divorce lawyer calls your office and tells you he represents the wife of a wealthy client. The attorney states that he has very damaging evidence against your client and that he intends to use it unless your client agrees to grant a quick, uncontested divorce and enters into a costly property settlement agreement. What is your opening move?

Every lawyer has his own list of war stories involving worried clients facing every sort of problem imaginable. In all but a handful of cases, negotiation plays the primary role in the ultimate resolution of the situation. In each instance, the lawyer must sort out the facts, identify the problem, and then make an opening move that will put the negotiation process in motion. Unfortunately, too many lawyers jump into action prematurely without giving sufficient attention to the overall objectives of the client and the consequences of their opening moves. Leaping before looking is common in a busy law practice, especially when the lawyer is being pressured by a panic-stricken client who wants action, *now!* While this response to a problem situation is certainly understandable, it often leads to disastrous results. When this occurs, it's the client who suffers and the lawyer who takes the blame.

GREEN DOESN'T NECESSARILY MEAN GO

The dilemma of exactly when and how to initiate a negotiation is much like being in a hurry to get to an appointment in your automobile only to be caught by a red light. You fidget impatiently while waiting for what seems like an eternity before the light changes color. As soon as you see green, your impulse is to charge ahead without looking to see if the other cars have honored the traffic signal. The result is a trip to an auto body shop and sometimes to the hospital. The lesson is clear. Just because the light is green does not necessarily mean you should go. The cautious driver will pause long enough to ascertain whether he can proceed safely. The negotiator should do the same.

RESTRAINT: THE FIRST RULE OF OPENING A NEGOTIATION

Despite the sense of immediacy that is generally associated with representing legal clients, restraint should be the first rule governing all opening move decisions. For example, just because another attorney phones your office and demands to speak to you about a pending matter doesn't mean it will be to your advantage to comply with his request. Just because a client is overly anxious to conclude an agreement in the shortest time possible doesn't mean it is in his best interest to do so. When it comes to making your opening move or responding to someone else's, always be guided by what is in your best interest rather than that of your adversary. If it means waiting a day or two, do it. On the other hand, if you see an opportunity to expedite a negotiation to your benefit, you should act accordingly. There is certainly no magic in delay merely for the sake of delay. However, pausing to assess the many implications of a specific move or proposal often leads to agreements and settlements based more on reason and less on reaction. The approach is always preferable to paying litigation counsel to deal with problems the negotiation should have resolved. Unfortunately, it's substantially easier to sell this approach to your client after the reality of the litigator's bill for services rendered has had time to register.

THE GIVEAWAY: BEWARE OF THIS COMMON OPENING MOVE BLUNDER

A common blunder that illustrates the negotiation axiom "stop, look and listen" is the "Giveaway." It usually goes like this: Your client has reached an agreement in principle with another firm regarding a business transaction. While the major points have been worked out, there are numerous issues of varying importance that are either up in the air or that haven't been addressed at all. Many of these issues are of no real consequence, while others are potentially troublesome. Rather than face up to these thorny issues, the two businessmen take the easy way out by deciding to "leave the details to the attorneys." In truth, they are leaving out not only details, but also some very controversial points that could prove fatal to the agreement.

A few hours after the agreement in principle has been reached, you receive a call from your client who is bubbling with optimism. He gives you a thumbnail sketch of the deal and tells you to expect a call from the other party's attorney to work out the details. He concludes the conversation by telling you it's all routine and that he is leaving for a well-earned week in Hawaii to celebrate his latest business success. Ten minutes later, the other attorney calls. After some obligatory smalltalk, you get down to business. The opposing attorney suggests that you resolve as many noncontroversial matters as possible so as to expedite preparation of the documents. Thinking this makes sense, you agree. He ticks off five or six points that his client would like your client to agree to. To each you respond with a "no problem" or "fine." Ten minutes into the conversation, he gets around to a zinger that your client probably never thought about but one that you know he shouldn't or wouldn't agree to. Cordiality quickly dissolves into confrontation as the first impasse develops. The conversation ends abruptly as you promise to run it by your client when he returns from Honolulu, knowing all the while that he will never agree to the other lawyer's proposal.

What is wrong with this approach? Simply this: The next time you call the attorney with requests that you feel are noncontroversial, you will most likely find him willing to agree, but only if you will make some concessions of your own. Suddenly, you realize that you have given away most of your trade points. As a result, you are faced with compromising a previously nonnegotiable point or, in the alternative, stonewalling the opposition, thus putting the entire deal in jeopardy. Either option leaves you at a disadvantage.

DON'T GET CAUGHT BY THE GIVEAWAY

In this example, the attorney could have avoided his dilemma easily by making himself unavailable to negotiate until he had time to review the entire deal with his client and formulate a negotiation plan that would have identified problem areas, trade points, fallback positions, and negotiating approaches. Unfortunately, this was not the case, thus allowing the opposing attorney, who had prepared his negotiating plan, to seize an initial advantage. Fortunately, this doesn't have to happen to you.

NINE COMMON OPENING MOVE TRAPS TO AVOID

The Giveaway is only one example of how a premature opening move can detrimentally affect a negotiation. Other common traps associated with failure to consider your opening move carefully include:

- Overreaction
- Saying too much
- Failure to verify important information
- Acting on insufficient information
- Failure to grasp points of procedure
- Inadequate preparation
- Revealing strategic plans
- Leverage positions
- Unwittingly tipping the opposition to your future moves.

Practice tip: As with the Giveaway, most of these pitfalls can be avoided by approaching a negotiation cautiously. A key phrase that will serve you well in constructing the appropriate opening move or response is "Reflect rather than react."

THE FIVE FUNCTIONS OF THE OPENING MOVE

Because the "Opening Move" sets the tone of a negotiation and can often play a crucial role in exerting and maintaining control, it is important to understand fully its functions and limitations. Generally speaking, you should try to accomplish the following five objectives when making your Opening Move:

1. Gather information
2. Build rapport
3. Balance perceptions
4. Define negotiations parameters
5. Make initial use of leverage

GATHER INFORMATION

The opening round of any negotiation can be very useful in gaining information about the opposition that can be evaluated and utilized at a later stage. This function of the opening move is absolutely essential for effective creation and use of leverage. It is also the only way to avoid the traps of miscalculation and taking action based on insufficient or erroneous information.

Initial conversations or exchange of correspondence can often reveal the opposition's negotiating objectives, leverage positions, and internal deadlines. They can also help identify the real decision makers, disclose points of procedure, and provide insight into the personalities of the opposition. All of these points of information are essential to completing the preparation phase of a given negotiation.

Practice tip: Beyond these points of essential information, any knowledge gained from the initial stages of the negotiation is potentially valuable. The more extensive your knowledge base, the better position you will be in to deal effectively with the opposition. It is imperative to learn as much as possible before formulating a position that may take the form of a binding offer or a response to an offer. A miscalculation based on insufficient or erroneous information is the stuff of which ulcers and lost clients are made.

Where to find the information you need: There are numerous techniques for using the initial stage of a negotiation to gather information.

The most obvious and often most effective is to ask, "What does your client want?"; "Who is making the final decision?"; "When do you have to know something?" A surprising number of unthinking lawyers will simply respond to your questions even when it might not be in their best interest to do so.

The "Get Acquainted" phone call or lunch: Another technique is the "Get Acquainted" phone call or lunch. This offers an opportunity to communicate with the other side in a relaxed atmosphere. You will likely pick up valuable bits of information and have a chance to assess the opposing attorney's personal negotiating style while having to reveal little of your own position or style.

Invite the opposition to make an offer: Other information-gathering techniques include inducing the other side to send a proposed contract draft or letter outlining the terms of an initial offer. Analyzing such documents can help provide information about the other party's positions without the risk of having to reveal your own prematurely.

Utilize standard sources of information: Martindale Hubble is always a good starting point for gaining insight into your opponent, just as *Dun and Bradstreet* and *Standard & Poors* are sources of information about various industries and executives that could be relevant to the transaction in question.

Check with your client: In many instances, your client will have access to knowledge or information that he may not think will be useful but that in fact could be highly relevant to some aspect of the negotiation. It often comes down to asking the right questions.

Information is the key to success: Regardless of whether a negotiation centers around a business acquisition, personal injury litigation, a collective-bargaining dispute, or any of a thousand and one conceivable topics, information is the key to your ultimate success. It will always be necessary to compile as much information as possible about the subject matter and personalities involved before you will be able to formulate an intelligent negotiation position and plan. We've all heard the horror stories about the attorney who settled a case for less than the claim was worth only because of insufficient or erroneous information. This is why doing your homework in the area of information gathering should be a primary objective of your Opening Move.

ESTABLISH A RAPPORT WITH THE OPPOSING COUNSEL

In the real world of practicing attorneys, the negotiation process is rarely a screaming battlefield of demands, threats, and ultimatums. In the first place, few negotiators possess such an overwhelming degree of bargaining strength needed to back up such an approach. Second, and more important, such an approach generally does little except to alienate the other party into finding an alternative to dealing with heavy-handed lawyers and clients. This is not to say that the Hardball approach doesn't exist or shouldn't be used in certain circumstances; however, in the great majority of cases it is simply inappropriate and not effective. Contrary to the way it may be depicted in fiction, most negotiations are based, at least to some degree, on a cooperative process where the emphasis is on compromise and problem solving. This is the essence of what has been discussed previously. A good, working rapport is absolutely essential if this approach is to succeed. This is why establishing a personal rapport with the opposing party and attorney is another important function of the Opening Move.

Don't confuse rapport with weakness: We caution you not to confuse rapport with behavior that could be perceived as a signal of weakness or uncertainty. The correct approach is to project a sense of natural ease and openness, balanced by self-confidence, efficiency, and firmness.

The problem of too much rapport: While a good rapport with the other lawyer is usually a plus factor, it can also be a potential stumbling block. This occurs when rapport turns into over-familiarity. This is a real problem in smaller communities and within certain concentrated industries where lawyers find themselves repeatedly negotiating with the same people. To make matters worse, they often encounter their negotiating counterparts just as frequently on the golf course or in the course of professional and community activities. In these instances, rapport is often already established, or in some cases has gone beyond the realm of possibility due to past battles not forgotten. If you find yourself in such a position, be on guard to avoid unconscious patterns that make you predictable, and resist the tendency to let personal feelings influence professional judgments. This is a very real problem in many sectors of practice. It can produce subtle, yet substantial negative repercussions at the bargaining table. Awareness is the only way to avoid this insidious enemy against your effectiveness.

Three Times Fore: To illustrate the problem, consider the unfortunate case of Mr. Fore. Mr. Fore is a very good plaintiff's lawyer practicing in a medium-size midwestern city. In the past, his only problem was predictability. Fore's standard operating procedure in personal injury cases was to demand approximately three times the amount for which he was willing to settle his case. The insurance defense bar privately nicknamed him "Three Times Fore" because they knew his bottom-line assessment of the case's worth as soon as he made his initial demand. Unfortunately for Mr. Fore, it took several years for him to realize what his opposition had already figured out. Fortunately for Mr. Fore, he was able to correct this habit, but not before it cost him and his clients a substantial amount of money in lost settlements over the years.

Practice tip: The problem of constantly negotiating with the same faces poses numerous opportunities to lose effectiveness at the bargaining table. Speaking too freely, failing to move aggressively, or letting down your guard with familiar adversaries are all realities facing any practicing attorney. It takes constant effort to combat this subtle and often unconscious form of negotiating ineffectiveness.

BALANCE PERCEPTIONS TO BUILD YOUR CREDIBILITY

When we speak of rapport with opposing counsel, we're not just referring to personal pleasantry. Building credibility and respect in the eyes of the opposing attorney is a critical factor to conducting an effective negotiation. Ideally, all lawyers and clients engaged in negotiation would be of equal age and reputation with each possessing the same relative degree of experience, ability, resources, and bargaining strength. We all know this is seldom the case. There will always be disparities, both real and perceived. The Opening Move is the time to balance these disparate perceptions. Failure to at least neutralize or partially offset negative perceptions at the outset will most likely result in a disjointed, defensive posture for the rest of the negotiation.

The young lawyer versus the old pro: Take the example of a young lawyer who is pitted against an old lawyer. The natural perception of the older attorney is that his counterpart is inexperienced, uncertain, and thus at a competitive disadvantage. On the other hand, the younger attorney will often assume that the older attorney is more knowledgeable and generally more competent to represent his client. Of course, these common assumptions are not always true; however, perceptions are what count. For this reason, the younger attorney must use the Opening Move to balance these disparities or perceived disparities. The correct initial approach by the younger lawyer is to be more reserved and formal than he might be with a lawyer his own age. His tone and substance should convey an image of self-confidence, firmness, and complete familiarity with the facts and law involved in the matter being discussed. He must also take every opportunity to convey subtly to his older opponent that his initial impressions were inaccurate. While, in many cases, this sense of calm, cool assuredness may be an act, it is essential that it be a convincing one in order to balance the perceptions held by the more experienced lawyer.

Prize fights and negotiations: The opening rounds of a negotiation are much like a prize fight. Each lawyer is probing for weaknesses that can be exploited later. Awareness of this process is essential in order to convey the right signals. If the opponent does not respect or trust you in the early stages of bargaining, you're in for some rough going in the later rounds. If he spots a weakness early, he is sure to exploit it later. If you give him an opening, he's likely to go for a knock-out punch. It is your job to prevent any of this from happening while sizing up the opposition for yourself.

Practice tip: Building a rapport, establishing respect and trust, and balancing negative perceptions should all be interwoven into your Opening Move. The key to achieving success in all of these areas is an ongoing awareness that while you should be probing the opposition, also know that the opposition is doing the same thing to you. This awareness should be followed with a projection of the "right" signals to your opponent. These signals will, of course, vary with the circumstances, personalities, and subject matter. Awareness and flexibility provide the one-two combination to get things off on the right foot.

DEFINE YOUR NEGOTIATION PARAMETERS

An important function of any opening move is to define the parameters of a particular negotiation. This simply means identifying the issues and objectives deemed important by the opposition as well as the outside limits or settlement range relating those issues. Of course, you will want to do as much of this as possible in the preparation phase; however, it is virtually impossible to appreciate the other side's position fully until you reach the Opening Move stage.

Buying and selling a widget factory: This concept is best explained by the following illustration. Assume two parties are negotiating for the sale and purchase of a widget factory. The prospective purchaser, a major corporation, is interested in two primary issues: price and time. It is willing to pay a reasonable amount, but is also willing to pass up the deal if the seller insists on making price demands that would endanger the long-term profitability of the acquisition. Time is important because the corporation is seeking to invest year-end profits in a major capital purchase prior to the end of its fiscal year so as to substantially reduce the company's tax liability. The prospective purchaser's fiscal year is due to end in forty-five days. The corporation's attorney has been authorized to pay up to $5 million in cash. However, corporate officials feel that $4.1 to $4.6 million is reasonable and that anything under $4 million would be a steal.

The prospective seller is the founder and president of Widget Manufacturing. By virtue of controlling 90 percent of the stock, he is able to make all decisions regarding the proposed sale. His primary objective is to get the most for his money in the shortest time possible. He especially wants to sell to this particular corporation because he feels they are capable of paying cash for the transaction. Unlike the prospective buyer, the seller has no predetermined internal deadline, yet he is eager to make a deal in the shortest time possible. He also knows that finding alternative buyers will be a time-consuming proposition. For this reason, he would be willing to wait six to eight weeks at the outside; however, the primary consideration is to consummate a cash deal with this buyer. He feels the company is worth between $4.5 and $5.5 million, but would be willing to accept as little as $3.75 million to ensure a quick deal.

In this hypothetical transaction, the deal points are almost identical for both buyer and seller. The settlement range or parameters set by the parties are illustrated by the following chart:

PARAMETERS			
ISSUES	BUYER	SELLER	SETTLEMENT RANGE
Time	Max—45 days Min—ASAP	Min—ASAP Max—40–60 days (flexible)	0—45 days
Money	Max—5.0 million Min—Reasonable (3.5) Terms—Cash	Min—$3.75 million Max—$5.50 million Terms—Cash	$3.75 million to $5 million Cash

In this situation, it is clear there is strong interest on both sides. For obvious reasons, neither party wants to reveal information that could be transformed into leverage and used against them.

In the initial stages of this negotiation, both attorneys will obviously probe for information with regard to time and price parameters. A careless remark or an unthinking response to a direct question could reveal this information. This will in turn give one of the parties an important leverage advantage.

Conduct and demeanor is another way to read the other party's negotiating parameters. Appearing too eager or pushing for a response is usually a clear signal of deadline pressure.

There will be times when it will be relatively easy to identify the other party's parameters without revealing your own. The question is what to do when it's not so easy, or conversely, how to respond tactfully to attempts aimed at eliciting such information.

MAKE US AN OFFER:
HOW TO SET UP THE FLOOR/CEILING TRAP

The oldest method of identifying negotiating parameters is inviting the other side to make an offer. This has the effect of creating either a ceiling or floor to the negotiation. For instance, suppose the attorney for the buyer invites his counterpart to disclose what the seller would be willing to accept? A low initial offer ($4.5 million) by the seller effectively establishes a ceiling. This tells the buyer that the maximum he would have to pay is half a million dollars below the authorized purchase price. This offer would also lead most people to believe that the ultimate purchase price could be lowered through more negotiation.

On the other hand, a high initial offer ($7 million) could be viewed as simply being beyond reality. In light of the time constraints, the buyer might feel it would be fruitless to pursue further negotiations and would begin to seek an alternative acquisition immediately.

In both examples, the party making the offer is at a disadvantage.

Two ways to escape the floor/ceiling trap: There are two solutions to this common dilemma. The first is to decline making an offer and invite the other side to make the first move. Sometimes this works. However, most times a game of "first offer ping-pong" ensues.

Talk in ranges rather than specifics: The other approach is to talk in terms of ranges. The seller's response would be something like this: "Well, we feel the company is probably worth in the neighborhood of $4.5 to $6 million." While this establishes a ceiling, it is a flexible one with plenty of room for give and take. Generally, this type of offer will elicit a response ranging from anger to disbelief— "I'm shocked"—to concurrence—"Well, that's probably a little high, but it's in the ballpark."

Practice tip: In this example, the repercussions of revealing parameters was potentially dangerous. There will be some negotiations where candor may be the best policy. The only guideline we offer is to assess your situation very carefully before choosing this approach.

You don't have to be held prisoner by your mistakes: In the event you unwittingly fall into the floor/ceiling trap or tip the other side as to time pressures, remember that this doesn't have to spell disaster. Negotiation has no rules except the ones you make or accept. Just because you make a low initial offer doesn't mean you have to be bound by it. The same is true of deadlines. Whenever practical, retract your offer and come in higher or find an alternate way to deal with your time pressures. While the circumstances won't always allow this, do it whenever possible. If you can't retract your offer and the consequences of a deal would be counterproductive, remember that your ultimate option is to walk away from the deal. You are always better off with no deal than with a bad deal.

INITIAL USE OF LEVERAGE

The last function of the Opening Move is the initial use of leverage. To illustrate, assume that the prospective buyer in our widget factory example knew the approximate price range that was acceptable to the seller. Also assume that the seller was eager for a quick cash deal. Based on this information, the buyer's attorney could invoke the leverage of timing and uncertainty by offering to buy the company for $4.5 million with 10 percent down and the balance financed with a ten-year payout. Alternatively, he could offer $3.75 million in cash with a fifteen-day closing as a condition precedent to the deal. In either event, the buyer would accomplish its objectives. If the seller chose the first option, the buyer would purchase the company for $500,000 less than it was willing to pay and would still have plenty of time to locate an alternative acquisition. If the seller selected option number two, which is much more likely under the circumstances, the buyer would be able to buy the company at a bargain price while also building in a time cushion to find an alternate acquisition should the seller have second thoughts.

Conversely, if the seller was privy to the buyer's internal deadline, he should convey strong interest in the deal without settling on a specific price. This would be accompanied by subtle delay tactics calculated on extending the negotiation beyond the point where it would be realistic for the buyer to seek an alternative acquisition. Once this point was reached, the seller could count on receiving a higher purchase price provided it is within the predetermined $5 million maximum figure authorized by the buyer.

This is only one illustration of how the Opening Move can be used to exert leverage. The variations are as numerous as the different fact situations that confront you and will largely be determined by how extensive your knowledge base is.

Caution: Opening move tactics cut two ways: The only word of caution here is to remember that tactics you use will surely be used against you. This is why any signal from the opposition should be analyzed and investigated as thoroughly as possible before a response is made. To this end, we reemphasize the caveat mentioned earlier in the chapter: "Reflect rather than react."

HOW TO MAKE THE OPENING MOVE

Almost every negotiation involving nonlawyers is initiated by one of three means: direct personal contact, telephone, or correspondence. Lawyers are uniquely endowed with a fourth means, the lawsuit. There is certainly no hard-and-fast rule as to which avenue is most effective. This will depend on the particular circumstances and personalities of the parties as well as the goals of the client and the negotiating styles of the parties. Each approach has its advantages and disadvantages. Let's look at each.

HOW TO HANDLE DIRECT PERSONAL CONTACT

The meeting, like typewriters and expense accounts, is a staple in the world of business and law. Whether the site is an office, restaurant, or golf course, this is often the best way to get the ball rolling, especially in a business setting. It usually starts with one lawyer making an offhand comment or overture to another lawyer or business executive that he has a client interested in establishing a business relationship provided terms and conditions could be worked out to everyone's satisfaction. The primary benefit of the direct approach is immediacy. In addition to establishing that the other party might be interested in the proposed deal, there is the opportunity for feedback and elaboration as well as the chance to observe the other person's reaction and demeanor. For this reason, the information function can be maximized through the personal meeting.

GUARD AGAINST THE DOWNSIDE OF PERSONAL CONTACT

The downside of the personal contact approach is the tendency to disclose too much or make ill-advised statements without time for investigation or reflection. This is especially true for the person to whom the proposal is being made. These potential dangers tend to be magnified in more relaxed settings such as over lunch or at a cocktail party. The best out is to "take it under advisement" and change the subject if you feel as if you **are** drifting into dangerous waters.

Beyond proposing a "deal," in a business setting, the personal approach is probably not the best vehicle for initiating a negotiation aimed at resolving conflict. This is especially true if the subject matter deals with controversial or potentially troubling issues or if litigation is a possible alternative to agreement.

POINTS TO KEEP IN MIND
WHEN MAKING AN OPENING
MOVE BY TELEPHONE

The telephone serves much the same function as the person-to-person approach, with several notable exceptions.

THE CALLER HAS CONTROL

The person calling is always able to control the initial subject matter and timing of the contact. Additionally, the caller enjoys an edge in preparation. Conversely, the person being called often falls victim to surprise and is rarely prepared to the same extent as the caller.

HOW TO COUNTER THE SURPRISE ELEMENT

The best way to counter the surprise element is simply to choose not to take the call. You can simply be "in a meeting," "in court," "busy," or "unavailable." Experienced legal secretaries have a marvelous facility for handling these situations with the utmost tact and cordiality. The rule governing use of the telephone to initiate a negotiation or to respond to an overture is to do it only when you consider it an opportunity. The Giveaway is a clear example of how an attorney was able to use the telephone to seize control of a negotiation to the detriment of someone totally unprepared to negotiate.

THE BENEFITS OF THE TELEPHONE

As with the meeting, the telephone can be an effective instrument when it comes to commencing a business-related negotiation. Because facial reactions can be concealed while allowing for immediate feedback, the telephone can sometimes prove effective in disputes involving potential litigation. A call to another lawyer can often help define issues, provide background information, and help establish a rapport without going into the substantive aspects related to the problem at hand. As with the potential downside risks inherent in the face-to-face meeting, preparation and self-control are essential so as not to disclose information prematurely or add to the level of hostility stemming from the dispute. Beyond these basic objectives, you are probably best advised to avoid the telephone until you have sufficient information to formulate a position.

ADDITIONAL POINTS FOR HANDLING
TELEPHONE NEGOTIATIONS

When the telephone is used, the following points should be kept in mind.

Take notes: Detailed note taking provides a record of the conversation. Commitments, concessions, and points of information can often get lost over the course of a protracted negotiation. A dated phone memorandum form in the file can be a potentially powerful leverage device, especially if the opposition attempts to modify earlier positions and understandings reached over the phone.

Use a telephone agenda list: How many times have you completed a telephone conversation only to realize that an important point was never discussed? A checklist of items to be discussed is a must before using the telephone to negotiate. This is the only effective way to ensure the call will be focused on the subject matter you want discussed.

Calculators, pens, and paper: These are three essentials that should always be close to your telephone. These items keep you organized and help you make or understand calculations that may be necessary to the conversation.

Resist pressure to respond: Because of the immediacy of the telephone, there is often pressure to respond to questions, positions, or offers. The dangers inherent in this type of behavior have already been discussed. Self-control is the only way to offset this human tendency. Remember, there is no rule that says you have to respond to anything. Often, the best approach is to say as little as possible or nothing at all.

HOW TO USE
CORRESPONDENCE EFFECTIVELY
IN THE OPENING MOVE

Correspondence plays an important role in all phases of negotiation. Its many uses and functions will be analyzed in succeeding chapters dealing with maintaining control, fallback techniques, and closing, as well as in a chapter devoted solely to correspondence. From the standpoint of the opening move, correspondence is most commonly used by lawyers in situations involving contested claims and potential litigation. The role of correspondence in business-related negotiations is generally reserved for later stages once the negotiation has been initiated. The primary exception of this is the "Dear John" business letter that is dispatched by the thousands every working day. It reads more or less as follows: "After careful consideration of your client's proposal, we feel it would be in our mutual best interests not to proceed at this time.... Thank you for considering us.... etc., etc., etc." Translation: "The answer is no."

THE DEMAND LETTER

The demand letter is the vehicle most lawyers use to initiate lawsuit settlement negotiations. Every mailman's bag contains a few of these in any given week. The demand letter serves several functions. First, it provides notice of a claim and advises the adversary that the claimant is being represented by an attorney. From a more subtle standpoint, the demand letter sets the tone for the negotiation. A well-drafted, detailed letter helps substantiate the plaintiff's demand while also communicating the lawyer's style, which helps build his credibility. A well-thought-out, carefully drafted letter summarizing the facts on which a case rests and concluding with a demand of varying specificity will be given much more serious consideration than a two-paragraph, bare-bones notice of representation, followed by an exorbitant demand. The latter variety of demand letter will most likely be ignored or treated by the opposition with varying degrees of hostility or amusement. The essentials of how to write an effective demand letter are discussed in detail in Chapter 8, which deals with correspondence.

WEIGH THE RISKS

As with anything else, there are downside risks associated with this Opening Move. First and most importantly, if you represent a plaintiff always remember the familiar axiom that the best defense is a good offense. You can rest assured that the defendant's lawyer will do his best to conjure up a counterclaim that invariably will carry a prayer for relief in excess of yours. Even if there is no counterclaim, there is no guarantee that the defendant will respond with anything more than a general denial. Credibility and burden of proof are two primary factors that will determine how eager the defense is to enter into any negotiations beyond disposing of the nuisance value of the suit.

Practice tip: For this reason, it's best to file lawsuits only after careful consideration of the implications. Using an ill-advised lawsuit to bluff the opposition into a settlement is a calling card for disaster. On the other hand, if your client has a strong claim, you will enhance your chances for a negotiated settlement by using the suit as leverage.

SUCCESS IS ULTIMATELY UP TO YOU

Regardless of the method used to initiate a negotiation, remember that its chances for success will depend largely on the circumstances of the case, your level of preparation, and most importantly your skill in executing the Opening Move. Knowing what to do certainly helps in this regard, but in the final analysis your level of success will be determined by your own legal and interpersonal skills. This is why there is simply no substitute for rolling up your sleeves and doing it.

Your personal skills combined with the opening move principles set forth in this chapter provide you with an irresistible combination that will allow you to seize control of more than your share of negotiations. While this doesn't guarantee an ideal result every time out, it sure beats the alternatives.

6

Maintaining Control at Every Stage of the Negotiation

A primary objective of the opening move is to gain control of the negotiation. Once this is accomplished, the emphasis should shift to maintaining control at every stage of the bargaining process. Control, like anything else worthwhile, doesn't just happen. It's the product of calculated, assertive actions designed to achieve predetermined objectives. This entails recognizing the type and degree of control needed for a given situation, followed by positive steps designed to realize your control objective.

NONSMOKING PLEASE

Control doesn't just happen. You have to make it happen; when you fail to assert yourself, you often will find yourself being controlled. This principle is best illustrated by the common and seemingly automatic process of airline seat selection. Most people who fly regularly have certain preferences regarding where they want to sit. If you don't smoke, don't like to be cramped, and like to look at the scenery, your requirements are fairly clear. Yet, how many times have you automatically replied "Nonsmoking" to the only question asked you by the boarding agent only to wind up feeling like a flying sardine wedged into the middle seat between a professional wrestler and a linebacker for the Dallas Cowboys. Your only consolation is not having to inhale someone else's cigarette smoke. Even this triumph loses its luster when you notice several rows of empty seats in a nearly deserted rear smoking section. This unfortunate situation could have been avoided simply by informing the agent that you also wanted a window seat where you could spread out. By not doing so, you relinquished control over an important aspect of the flight that is already costing you hundreds of dollars. For that kind of money, it's not unreasonable to want to be comfortable. To make matters worse, the agent most likely would have honored your request had you only spoken up.

ASSERTING YOURSELF IS A KEY TO CONTROLLING A NEGOTIATION

Speaking up is a key to asserting control over a negotiation. If your opponent suggests a meeting at an inconvenient time, simply tell him you're tied up. If you are trying to establish a place to negotiate, don't hesitate to suggest your preference rather than automatically responding with a "you name it" or "anywhere is fine with me." Failure to speak up is an example of failing to seize opportunities to exert control over various elements of the negotiation.

This is not to suggest that controlling a negotiation is always as simple as just expressing your preference, though it often can be. There will be times when it will either be inappropriate, unfeasible, or simply impossible to assert the type or degree of control you would like. However, an awareness of what you want to accomplish followed by steps to achieve your objectives will generally make a marked difference when it comes to totalling up the bottom line. Because control plays such an important role in your ultimate success, it is valuable to focus on specific control techniques that can be utilized in every negotiation situation you might encounter.

WHERE EFFECTIVE CONTROL BEGINS—CHOOSING THE TIME AND PLACE TO NEGOTIATE

You can gain an immediate advantage over your opponent by controlling when and where a negotiation will be conducted. Definite tactical and psychological advantages flow to the negotiator capable of controlling these seemingly insignificant factors. Surprisingly, as the previous example suggests, many attorneys allow their opponents to gain the upper hand by surrendering control of these tactical aspects of bargaining. Forfeiting an opportunity to exert control over time and place is often the first step to letting the process control you. Fortunately, this is a mistake that can often be avoided by simply taking the initiative to suggest a time and place to negotiate, or, conversely, by not automatically agreeing to any proposal the opposing attorney may suggest.

MY OFFICE OR YOURS?

Most negotiators perform their work with greater confidence and efficiency in a familiar setting. Consequently, you're apt to be more relaxed and mentally sharper if you are able to conduct a negotiation in your own office or other comfortable and familiar surroundings. In addition to comfort and familiarity, the negotiator with the home office advantage has complete control over the temperature, lighting, seating arrangement, scheduled breaks, use of assistants, and presence or absence of interruptions. On the other hand, the visitor is subjected to an array of unfamiliar circumstances that makes it more difficult for him to perform at optimum levels.

The value of the home office advantage is well illustrated by an emotion-charged property settlement and custody negotiation incident to a divorce. The very nature of any contested domestic matter is the cause for a great deal of tension and anxiety. An attorney can raise the anxiety level by scheduling the opposing party's deposition at his office. The fear of the unknown coupled with an unfamiliar setting will likely cause the deposed party to experience extreme anxiety as the deposition date nears. This heightened anxiety may result in the opponent granting concessions or agreeing to less desirable settlement terms just to avoid the unpleasant confrontation. Additionally, the added edge of a familiar environment can help you and your client deal with the situation from a position of strength and security in contrast to the uncertainty and anxiety the opposition is experiencing.

ONE INSTANCE WHEN YOUR OPPONENT'S OFFICE IS PREFERABLE

There is one instance based on tactical considerations that may dictate negotiating in your opponent's office instead of your own. If you have decided to employ anger coupled with a walk-out tactic, it would be easier to play out this move if you are negotiating in your opponent's office rather than your own.

While this tactic is rarely employed, it can prove useful in extreme situations.

HOME AWAY FROM HOME

If you are unable to persuade your opponent to negotiate at your office, attempt to schedule another location favorable to you. For example, if your opponent is reluctant to come to your office to negotiate, invite him to lunch at your business club where you will still feel at home. If you are still unsuccessful, invite your opponent to lunch at a restaurant that is mutually agreeable or to a business club where both of you are members. The key is to maintain your comfort and familiarity level whenever possible.

HOW TO OFFSET YOUR OPPONENT'S
HOME OFFICE ADVANTAGE

Always try to avoid your opponent's office unless you have a tactical reason for going there or unless you simply have no choice. When you are forced to negotiate at your opponent's office, you should take steps to offset his advantage. This can be done by visiting your opponent's office to discuss less important issues. After one or two visits, you will have acquired a feel of the surroundings, thereby reducing your opponent's advantage when crucial aspects of the negotiation will be decided.

Practice tip: Whenever it's necessary for your client to accompany you into unfamiliar territory, try to remove as much of his uncertainty as possible by describing what he will encounter and what will probably happen. Your client will not only appreciate your efforts, but will perform much better if you take the time to brief him. Remember, for many clients, a visit to your office is difficult enough; a trip to the opposing lawyer's office can be an ordeal.

TAKING YOUR CUE TO ASSERT CONTROL

As our airline seat selection example suggests, too many negotiators fail to realize the importance of seizing the initiative in a negotiation. Whenever the opposing lawyer makes statements such as:

"Does it make any difference to you where we meet?"
"Where do you want to take her deposition?"

"My office or yours?"

"We need to discuss this matter—what about meeting at my office?"

You should instinctively take your cue to seize the opportunity he has created. Even if the actual advantage gained is negligible, making a habit of speaking up helps develop the assertiveness necessary to take charge of other aspects of the negotiation process consistently.

HOW ABOUT 8:30 MONDAY MORNING?

How do you normally feel at 8:30 every Monday morning? If you're like most people, probably not so great. Then why would anyone agree to negotiate at this time or for that matter any time when they are not capable of functioning at maximum efficiency? Ironically, many attorneys spend countless hours preparing for a negotiation, only to give the other side the advantage by routinely saying yes when the voice on the other end of the telephone line asks, "How about 8:30 Monday morning?"

CONTROLLING INTERNAL AND EXTERNAL SCHEDULES

Everyone has a certain time of day when they are at their peak. For some, the morning hours are the most productive. Others are at their best in the afternoon, while some prefer evening hours. Alternatively, everyone has some time during every day or week when they don't operate at peak efficiency. Generally, Monday mornings and Friday afternoons are not the most productive times of a work week. In addition, everyone finds their schedule bottlenecked at various times, which in turn makes completing ordinary tasks more difficult. Using your peak time for important negotiations is another way to assert control over a negotiation. Surprisingly, in the vast majority of situations your choice of date and time for a negotiation will be accepted without any argument from your opponent. By taking the initiative, you will find that most meetings, telephone conversations, depositions, and trial dates can be scheduled to suit your timeframe.

Practice tip: A key factor in control is awareness. Be aware of what time of the day and week on your schedule is right for you, then suggest it to your opponent as a matter of course. When your opponent does the same, don't throw away a potential advantage by indifferently agreeing to a suggestion that would not prove beneficial.

SEIZING UNSCHEDULED OPPORTUNITIES

Sometimes unscheduled opportunities to negotiate may occur at places and times that would normally not be advantageous for you. If the advantage of the moment outweighs the disadvantages, seize the opportunity. For example, assume you just spent the entire day working on a pending case in anticipation of contacting the opposing attorney the next day to discuss settlement approaches. By the end of the workday, you are quite knowledgeable of the case and have formulated your negotiation strategy. Pleased with your efforts, you stop off at the YMCA for a workout that leaves you feeling energetic and relaxed. As you are leaving the locker room, you meet the attorney whom you intend to contact the next day. It's apparent from his opening remarks that he would like to discuss the case right now. Should you? If you believe the advantages of the moment outweigh the traditional disadvantages, by all means proceed to negotiate. In this example, the advantages of a receptive opponent coupled with being well prepared, mentally and physically alert, and in a relaxed atmosphere far outweigh not being able to discuss the case in your office or at your prime time.

Practice tip: Flexibility should always be the watchword. Opportunity often presents itself when you least expect it. If you are in a position to seize the opportunity, do it. If you're not, chances are that the opportunity is one for your opponent rather than yourself. If this is the case, you would be best advised to avoid the issue until the time is right.

THE NEGOTIATOR'S SPEEDOMETER: THREE TECHNIQUES FOR PACING NEGOTIATIONS

There are three primary control ploys you can use to regulate the tempo of any negotiation. They are:

- Deadlock
- Delay
- Acceleration

One of these three pacing techniques should fit any situation that may confront you. For instance, certain advantages emanate from a rapid or fast-paced negotiating tempo. In this situation you would want to use acceleration tactics to speed up the bargaining process. Conversely, there are distinct advantages to using delay or deadlock tactics. Regardless of the tempo that is appropriate to your particular circumstances and objectives, one of these tactical approaches will enable you to assert some degree of control over the tempo of the negotiation. This enables you to coordinate the right moves with the proper timing. Unquestionable, smartly executed moves get results. However, the combination of the right move made at the right time can have a synergistic effect in terms of gaining the upper hand over the opposition. The pacing techniques discussed in this section will help you regulate the tempo of a negotiation so that you can derive maximum benefits from each move you make.

DEADLOCK—THE 5:00 RUSH-HOUR PLOY

Have you ever been caught in 5:00 rush-hour traffic in a large city? As you know, it can be a most frustrating experience. There's something about those endless lines of vehicles creeping toward their destinations that seems to frustrate everyone. As you become frustrated and irritated by the traffic jam, emotions run high and tempers flare. As bad as this situation seems, it can get much worse by adding one variable—a deadline.

Imagine the same traffic jam scene on a Friday afternoon as you attempt to reach the airport to catch your flight back home after a long business trip. Your frustration level is at its peak as you impatiently wait for the traffic to start moving. The additional pressure brought on by the deadline has a multiplier effect on your frustration level. Frustration mounts with each passing moment. Your anger is slowly replaced by a feeling of helplessness. This is exactly the effect deadlock has on most negotiators.

Negotiators fear deadlock because of the negative overtones associated with it. Deadlock seems to be synonymous with no agreement. To most negotiators, failure to agree means objectives are not met and goals are unrealized. Conclusion: The negotiators have failed, and therefore, must not be good negotiators. Unfortunately, those negotiators who have this misconception about deadlock have thrown away one of the most powerful negotiating weapons.

The use of deadlock can bring the entire negotiating process to a halt. It is a sure way to create the ultimate traffic jam in a negotiation. If your goal is to stop the bargaining process in midstream, deadlock will do the job. As a general rule, when your position will not be damaged by maintaining the status quo, deadlock can be used to stop the negotiating process so that the passage of time may uncover or create a weakness in your opposition.

HOW TO USE DEADLOCK IN THE NO-ACTION SITUATION

Charles Williamson is a three-year veteran of the National Football League. As a relatively low draft selection, he had to overcome a great deal of competition to earn a slot on the team in his rookie year. His dedication and determination enabled him to beat the cut and make the final team roster just prior to the regular season. Charles entered into a three-year contract with the team at a base salary of $55,000 per year in addition to the standard fringe benefits and other compensation incentives. Charles is now in his final year of the three-year contract and he is eagerly awaiting negotiation of a new contract. Fortunately for Charles, he has been a solid performer for the team and is well liked by the coaching staff and other team members. The general manager of the team made it known to Charles that he was willing to discuss contract terms anytime Charles was ready. Charles was fully aware that his marginal position during his rookie year affected his salary. As expected, Charles was eager to negotiate a better deal.

The general manager begins talking to Charles during summer camp about the new contract. The discussions are cordial and candid. The general manager is quick to agree with Charles that a salary increase is in order; however, no definite figures are offered by either side. The general manager is successful in disposing of all the less controversial secondary points that Charles agrees are minor in importance. Just prior to the start of the regular season, the parties get to the heart of the contract. Charles finally reveals his salary demands. Not surprisingly, the general manager expresses shock at such a demand. After the initial demand and counteroffer, it appears that Charles and the general manager are still $40,000 per year apart.

At this point, the general manager could attempt to close the gap between Charles' demands and the team's offer by further talks. But, since all the new contract points have been resolved except for salary terms, and since Charles will have to play out the current season under his old contract, the general manager is content with the status quo and decides to use deadlock as a ploy to close the salary gap.

The general manager tells Charles, "I'm prepared to raise my last offer by $10,000 per year, but that is as high as I can go. Charles, I'm sorry I can't do better, but with rising costs this is the best the team can do. After all, it's almost double what you are being paid now. In fact, I will even make the new contract effective immediately so you can earn more money starting with this Sunday's game. Please give it serious consideration—it's my final offer."

The general manager has put the burden to act squarely on Charles. Under the terms of the new offer, each week Charles delays in making a decision he loses money and the general manager saves money, or so it seems. Now Charles is faced with either substantially reducing his demands in order to get closer to what appears to be the team's final offer, or accepting the risks associated with becoming a free agent at the end of the season.

On the other hand, the general manager has chosen deadlock hoping that the passage of time might afford him a negotiating advantage. For instance, should Charles become injured during the season his future value might be impaired. The same is true if Charles doesn't perform well during the season or if a college player becomes a prospect for Charles' position. The occurrence of any of these events would diminish the value of Charles' services to the team. If Charles has an outstanding year, the general manager could always capitulate and pay the demanded salary. However, chances are that three out of four of the previously mentioned future contingencies will go against Charles, thus diminishing his bargaining strength. As a result, the general manager is content to accept deadlock, for the time being.

DELAY: MAKING TIME YOUR ALLY

Delay tactics are much more subtle than deadlock ploys, yet their objective is the same—to control the tempo of the negotiation in order to gain an advantage. Generally, delay tactics should be used when the passage of time will weaken your opponent's position or improve yours. For example, if your client has just been sued and has instructed you to settle prior to trial, when should you make the initial settlement offer? The initial settlement offer could be made immediately after receiving notice of the lawsuit, however this might be viewed as a sign of weakness by the opposition. Delaying your settlement offer until after a responsive pleading has been filed will put you in a more advantageous bargaining position.

Practice tip: Your negotiation posture could be further strengthened if a counterclaim were filed as part of your response. This represents a combination of defensive delay and offensive leverage.

DON'T CONFUSE DELAY WITH PROCRASTINATION

Delay should not be confused with procrastination. In the negotiator's world, delay is used as a calculated tactical device to gain a specified advantage over the opposition. Procrastination is neither planned nor calculated. It is a habit of postponing doing something until a future time because of laziness or indifference. In some situations, it may appear that an opponent is procrastinating when in fact he is using a well-camouflaged delay tactic.

BUYING TIME THROUGH DELAY

If your opponent is eager to move forward, delay is a good way to slow the tempo, thus allowing you to find out why he is in such a hurry. Generally, the other side will have a reason for stepping up the pace of bargaining. It will usually be advisable to find out why. Delay tactics can buy the time needed to do this.

Most attorneys are experts at using delay tactics. This is partially a byproduct of our complex and overworked legal system, which is quite susceptible to delay. Procedural delay can often be used to your clients' advantage. Consider the client who has been sued on an open account. He readily admits that he owes the plaintiff money, but he needs time to raise the money. By filing suit, the plaintiff has in effect given the defendant time to come up with the money by placing the case in the legal pipeline. The process takes time, and time is exactly what the defendant wants. Ultimately, in this case, the defendant will pay the plaintiff what he owes, but not before he is unwittingly granted extra time by the plaintiff's lawsuit.

USING ACCELERATION TO BRING MATTERS TO A CONCLUSION

Acceleration is the opposite of deadlock. This control tactic is used when the negotiator wants to speed up the process to take advantage of circumstances favorable to him.

Acceleration is an action-oriented tactic that can be used by the plaintiff as well as defense attorneys. Frequently, acceleration ploys are used by attorneys who prefer an aggressive negotiating style. These lawyers like to keep the pressure on and bring matters to a head. Acceleration tactics are well suited to this style of negotiation.

One example of acceleration is the attorney who is quick to file suit without issuing any advance warning. His main objective seems to be getting the case to trial as quickly as possible. Each stage of the negotiation is accelerated to the next, with the ultimate objective being the trial. The objective of acceleration is the same as deadlock and delay—to control the negotiation. Often acceleration is used to change the status quo. For instance, in a paternity dispute where the mother of an illegitimate child has been unsuccessful after numerous attempts to persuade the putative father to help in the support of the child, the attorney for the mother may decide it best to depart from his standard practice of issuing a demand letter to the potential defendant. Consequently, he decides to accelerate the process by foregoing the letter and filing suit immediately. Matters could be further accelerated by refusing to discuss settlement terms until the discovery phase of the litigation is completed. In an extreme situation, acceleration can be taken to the limit by refusing to discuss settlement terms until the day of trial.

Practice tip: Acceleration causes action. It is a useful tactic for maintaining control because it forces your opponent to respond to your moves. This forces the opposition into a defensive posture. The result is control of the negotiation.

HOW TO USE BALANCING
AS A CONTROL DEVICE

Balancing deals with the negotiator's continuing efforts to maintain a favorable bargaining posture, or, at the very least, to preserve a position of equilibrium. As long as the balance of power can be maintained, a negotiator can work from a relatively secure position. However, if the balance of power shifts in favor of one negotiator, the other is forced to deal from a position of weakness. Until the balance of power is restored, each move the disadvantaged negotiator makes takes on the appearance of a rear-guard action—certainly not the position of strength.

The need for balancing is ongoing. Concessions gained during the early rounds of a negotiation can be completely or partially lost or their value severely diluted if you are forced to deal from a position of weakness for too long. Consequently, the need to constantly maintain the balance of power with the opposition in order to preserve control is always present at every stage of the negotiation.

THE TWO RULES OF BALANCING

The balancing concept embraces two simple rules: "Don't let your opponent gain the upper hand at any stage of a negotiation," and, "If an opponent gains the upper hand, move quickly to bring the balance of power into a state of equilibrium."

For instance, if an opponent offers some startling new facts or a surprise witness during settlement negotiations of a case, control may be temporarily lost. Before you make any settlement proposal, control should be regained or, at least, balanced. This can be done by coming forward with some new information, facts, witnesses, or law of your own. Meeting threats with counterthreats or answering uncertainty with more uncertainty are additional illustrations of balancing.

Control is rarely lost by a single dramatic move on the part of the opposition. In the usual case, control ebbs away slowly. Failure to offset a shift in momentum can establish an irreversible trend in favor of the other side. Taking steps to recapture balance as the negotiation unfolds is the best way to maintain the necessary degree of control in the bargaining process.

PERSONAL INJURY NEGOTIATION: THE CLASSIC EXAMPLE OF
BALANCING

Personal injury cases are often classic examples of balancing in
action. Consider the usual chain of events in a personal injury case.
Someone is injured due to the negligence of another. The negligent
party is covered by liability insurance. Consequently, the insurance
company has exclusive control over settlement of the injured person's
claim during the early stages of the negotiation.

Once the injured person passes through the life-threatening or
acute pain phases, concern about receiving payment from the
negligent party emerges. Frequently, this concern for compensation
is motivated either by revenge or some idea that the plaintiff will reap
a windfall. In these types of cases, the injured party develops a very
high expectation level regarding the potential settlement value of his
claim. That expectation level is often based on emotional considerations, unrealistic perceptions, or just good old-fashioned misinformation that bear little or no relevance to the actual liability or
damages involved. If the injured person attempts to negotiate with
the insurance company at this stage, settlement talks usually tend to
break down due to positions adopted by the parties. At this stage, the
insurance company has control over the negotiation. Why? Because
they are in the business of disposing of claims; consequently, they
enjoy a superior knowledge base. The insurance company has a good
feel for what an inexperienced claimant, unrepresented by counsel, is
likely to do or not to do.

In our personal injury example, the insurance company is aware
of the injured party's unrealistic demands and is content with holding
its position by making an extremely low counteroffer. At this point
in the negotiation, the claimant has gained nothing from the insurance company but sympathy and a take-it-or-leave-it settlement offer
that is well below his expectation level. Many unskilled negotiators
who try to settle their claim without an attorney would most likely
view such a position as hopeless and agree to accept whatever
amount the insurance company offers. Consequently, the negotiation
ends. Score another victory for the insurance company.

In this scenario, the injured party never had control. Therefore,
his settlement demand never had enough impact to influence the
bargaining to a higher level. The result: a poor settlement for the
plaintiff.

TILTING THE BALANCE OF POWER

Assume the injured person engages the services of an attorney. Once the attorney explains the law controlling negligence actions, outlines the settlement process, explains such concepts as jury verdict expectancy and the time value of money, along with the settlement propensities of the subject insurance company, the injured party is in a much better position to evaluate the strengths and weaknesses of his case. Based on this information, a realistic expectation level and reasonable settlement range for negotiation purposes can be adopted.

By engaging an attorney, the injured party is able to bring the balance of power back into a state of equilibrium. Depending on the competency and reputation of the attorney, this in itself might be enough to tilt the balance of power in favor of the injured party. While the short-term effect is to give the plaintiff a boost, the lawyer and the insurance company know that the game has only just begun.

After several offers and counteroffers are generated by the injured party's attorney, the insurance company makes its last and final offer. Normally, the final offer is well below the amount demanded. At this point, the injured party is subjected to the lure and uncertainty of the last and final offer. In many instances, the enticement of the check in hand coupled with the uncertainty of forthcoming litigation will cause many clients and attorneys to accept the "purported" final offer. On the other hand, it must be pointed out that acceptance of an insurance company's offer at this stage might be prudent depending on the facts surrounding a case. In our example, if the plaintiff's attorney allowed the insurance company to maintain control throughout the early stages of the negotiation, the last and final offer will be quick in coming and low in amount. Alternatively, if plaintiff's counsel has maintained a balance of power, the insurance company will be much slower in issuing an ultimatum, and when it does the amount will be greater than in situations where control has been lost. If the balance of power has been tilted in favor of one negotiator for an extended period of time, odds are that he will usually be the one making the last and final settlement offer—not receiving it.

BALANCING AND COUNTERBALANCING

It is important to recognize the role that balancing played in this personal injury scenario. At the beginning of the negotiation, the expectation level of the injured party was extremely high due to emotionalism, unrealistic perceptions, and misinformation. Consequently, the insurance company enjoyed a power advantage at this stage due to its superior knowledge and experience. The company's position was reflected by its low settlement offer to the injured party. At this stage, the injured party was able to strengthen his position by retaining an attorney and thus acquiring additional information and knowledge about the settlement process. In essence, the injured party was able to bring the balance of power back into a state of equilibrium or balance. The balance of power tilted back in favor of the insurance company when it made its last and final offer. The injured party and his attorney were subjected to the enticement of the alleged last chance to settle without having to engage in costly and time-consuming litigation. Let's assume the insurance company's bluff was called and suit was instituted by the injured party. By filing suit, the balance of power was restored and possibly tilted in favor of the plaintiff depending on the specific law and facts involved. This balancing process continued with the filing of responsive pleadings, and trial motions and taking depositions. Throughout the process, the respective confidence levels of the parties were subjected to a continued ebb and flow that was ultimately reflected in the bottom line of the final settlement agreement.

THE IMPORTANCE OF CONTROLLING INTENSITY

The ability to control the intensity of a negotiation is often just as important as being able to control the pace of the bargaining process. For instance, consider the control strategy of a union labor leader seeking to negotiate a new agreement with management. At their first meeting, the labor leader announces his intention to call a strike if an agreement cannot be reached before a specified deadline. Such a ploy is a highly intensive way of attempting to gain and maintain control over the bargaining process. The union position could be further intensified by making an announcement at a press conference held immediately before the opening meeting with management. Here, the labor leader has used intensity to dramatize his union's demands and rally the support of the rank and file. It also has the effect of drawing the battle lines with the opposition. While such an approach can represent an intensive and provocative approach to negotiation, there are times when the circumstances require this type of aggression.

To contrast the union leader's highly intensive approach, consider a diplomat of a strategically important nonaligned Third World nation attempting to gain support for a sensitive proposition advocated by his country. Here, the circumstances call for a more oblique approach to bargaining to avoid the negative fallout from an adverse reaction. Lowering the intensity level is a vital consideration that will affect how the diplomat approaches his task.

Attorneys use these two intensity extremes and everything in between on a daily basis. The typical example of a low-intensity control tactic is a letter suggesting a course of action that is not backed up with any threat of suit or deadline for action. Conversely, a demand letter incorporating a threat of suit along with a "short fuse" deadline (ten days or less) would illustrate the use of a more intensive control tactic. The attorney's ability to read a situation and respond with the appropriate intensity will go a long way in affecting the bottom-line success or failure of the negotiation.

CONTROLLING FOCUS TO KEEP THE NEGOTIATION ON TRACK

Besides controlling pace and intensity, a third target for control relates to the focus of the negotiation. How many times have you been engaged in a conversation with friends only to see the subject of the discussion meander repeatedly. This phenomenon is an illustration of a failure of the parties to control the focus of the conversation. In most casual conversations, there is little need to control focus. In a negotiation, the ability to control focus can be of paramount importance.

TWO SUBTLE TECHNIQUES TO HELP YOU CONTROL FOCUS

Throughout any negotiation, there are two communication techniques that can be used to help you control the focus of a negotiation. They are *repetition* and *listening*. These simple and subtle techniques can be used in every conceivable negotiating situation. While both may appear of minor importance, don't be fooled. They can be very important when it comes to keeping a negotiation on track.

Even though repetition and listening are both communication techniques, they employ completely opposite approaches. Repetition is a technique used to send information. Conversely, listening is a technique used to receive information. When used together, they become an extremely powerful control device. Let us examine each in more detail.

REPETITION, REPETITION, REPETITION

During a complex negotiation, it is not uncommon for the negotiators to become bogged down in discussing collateral issues. As any family law practitioner will attest, parties to a domestic dispute often lose sight of their main objective—getting a divorce— and make every collateral point a deal point. Trying to reach a negotiated settlement when the parties subordinate their main objective each time a secondary issue is confronted can be a nightmare for any attorney. Repetition is an effective way to control such situations.

Repetition can help the negotiator do two things:

• Focus the opponent on your objective;
• Emphasize your strong points, or your opponent's weak points.

Repetition reminds. Consequently, both the sender and receiver are constantly reminded of the issue at hand. Repetition keeps your main objective foremost in the opponent's mind, making it much more difficult for primary issues to be sidetracked.

Successful use of repetition requires subtlety. It should not be employed by repeating standard phrases in a mechanical manner. Instead, the desired point or issue should be injected throughout the negotiation by subtle as well as obvious statements. When used properly, your opponent should have no doubt as to the issues that comprise the parameters of the negotiation.

Repetition also serves to emphasize and reinforce. Both plaintiff and defense attorneys use repetition during trial to emphasize to the judge or jury the strengths of their case or the weaknesses of their opponent's case. The repeated reminders of one's strength or an opponent's weaknesses not only have a persuasive effect on the judge or jury but also on the opponent.

Repetition can also be used as a way to exert leverage of uncertainty over an opponent. After being told of the weaknesses of a case, everyone, including your opponent, may begin to believe it. For instance, settlement negotiations involving a personal injury claim. The first move any defense lawyer usually makes is to tell the opposing attorney why the plaintiff doesn't have a strong enough case to merit the amount demanded. The defense attorney will magnify his opponent's weak points while emphasizing the client's strong points to cause doubt and uncertainty in the opponent. Repetition is useful in promoting the uncertainty that exists in the opposition's position throughout the negotiation.

THE ART OF LISTENING

Listening is another helpful communication technique that can be used to control the focus of a negotiation. To listen closely to what someone is saying takes concentrated effort. There is a natural tendency to interject a comment or idea without letting the person who is talking complete his statement. As a result, the would-be listener spends more time preparing a response than he does listening to what the person has to say. As a result, the listener fails to hear a portion of the message. This opens the door to misunderstandings and problems rather than to solutions.

Real listening requires disciplined concentration. This can prove to be a considerable challenge. Development of good listening habits will allow you to ferret out relevant information and ask probing questions designed to cut through the verbiage and get to the problem. Sustained active listening is by no means easy, but it is essential to your success as a communicator. Failure to listen actively is the quickest way to let the negotiation's focus stray to secondary issues or, worse yet, issues you have no interest in pursuing.

Even if the negotiation stays focused on the issues you deem important, failure to listen to and understand the other side will impede your ability to reach workable solutions acceptable to all concerned.

7

Tactical Negotiating Ploys That Can Improve Your Bargaining Position

In every negotiation, the participants are continually making moves and countermoves designed to improve their own relative positions. These tactical moves and countermoves are referred to as "ploys." Every negotiation is characterized by numerous ploys. Some prove highly effective, others do not. Some negotiators use ploys without any specific reason or well-defined plan. On the other hand, consistently successful negotiators are adept at utilizing ploys designed to achieve specific, predetermined objectives. Regardless of the particular situation in which you find yourself, ploys are a vital part of every negotiation. From ordinary domestic quarrels to disputes between world powers, everybody uses ploys. This chapter is devoted to discussing time-tested ploys that you can put to work in your law practice starting today.

DEADLINES: THE BASIS FOR MANY EFFECTIVE TACTICAL PLOYS

We briefly alluded to deadlines in our discussion of the leverage of timing. Deadlines are also the basis for a number of effective tactical ploys.

Deadlines motivate people to take action. As deadlines near, pressure mounts and decisions become mandatory. Action is required. Due to the nature of the legal system, attorneys are constantly working under the pressure of deadlines. Regardless of whether a deadline is imposed by a court or an opposing attorney, it effectively pushes cases and transactions to conclusion. As attorneys quickly learn, some deadlines are extremely flexible while others are rigid and uncompromising. For example, an appeal deadline imposed by a state statute is certainly a deadline that must be taken seriously. This kind of deadline will keep a lawyer in the office late at night and over

the weekend in order to comply with its time requirement. On the
other hand, an informal deadline imposed in a demand letter from an
opposing attorney that threatens suit unless some action is taken by a
certain date is a flexible time demand that would not normally cause
as great a degree of concern.

DEADLINES IN ACTION

Deadlines are useful in promoting action because they exert
pressure on the negotiating process. For instance, assume you desire
to apply maximum pressure on an opponent. This can be accomplished by setting deadlines that are regulated by the court or some
other independent authority which will have ultimate control over
determination of the case. Once a deadline is set in accordance with
the rules of the court or other authority, maximum pressure can be
leveled at your opponent by simply refusing to consent to his request
to alter the timetable. In most instances, attorneys are liberal in
granting voluntary extensions of time and other procedural modifi-
cations to opponents when such action is permissible. But in those
situations where the objective is to apply maximum pressure on your
opponent, remain steadfast and refuse to modify the official rules.
While such action will undoubtedly eliminate the possibility of
reciprocal favors from your opponent, it will subject him to a
pressurized situation, causing him to act. Under these circumstances,
such action is likely to be to your advantage.

Practice tip: For maximum effect, couple your deadline demand
with sanctions imposed by some higher authority. If the deadline is
not adhered to, remain uncompromising in your stand.

Informal deadlines: Informal deadlines are used regularly by
attorneys in their dealings with opposing attorneys and their clients.
An informal deadline is a pronouncement by one party that some
specified action be taken within a stated time period. Informal
deadlines are imposed or dictated by the opposition in an effort to
advance the case toward resolution. If these demands are not satisfied,
the party making them promises to respond with some type of
sanction. Basically, there are two forms of informal deadlines—the
short-fuse and the flexible deadline.

Short-fuse deadlines: If your objective is to spark immediate
action, attach a short fuse to your deadline. For example, instead of

giving the opposing party thirty days to respond to your demand letter, shorten the fuse to ten days or less. To enhance the credibility of your deadline, be prepared at the time the deadline is announced to take the threatened action immediately if response is not made within the given time. For instance, when writing a demand letter in connection with collection of an open account, advise the debtor he has "ten days to make payment or the attached lawsuit will be filed." The debtor realizes that the threat of suit is real. Why? Because he can see the complaint that will include a demand for attorney's fee, pre- and post-judgment interest and court costs in addition to the principal amount due the creditor. The attached complaint legitimizes the deadline threat. The work has already been done. Pressure mounts. The debtor realizes that his inaction will result in suit being filed. To avoid suit, he will have to act.

Using short-fuse deadlines brings a sense of immediacy to the informally imposed deadline. Whenever possible, support your threat with some documentation that action will be taken if the deadline is not met. The short fuse should never exceed ten days; otherwise, it will lose its effectiveness. Allowing the opponent too much time defuses the power of deadline. Time releases pressure. A sense of urgency will be sacrificed. This is why the fuse must remain short.

Practice tip: To enhance short-fuse deadlines, keep the response time to ten days or less and always be prepared to follow through with your threat immediately if the deadline is not met.

Flexible deadlines: The flexible deadline is well suited for situations where you want to press your opponent but are not yet prepared to take drastic action. The flexible deadline is imposed by extending the opponent's response time beyond ten days (e.g., fourteen days, thirty days, ninety days) or by using language in the demand designed to promote flexibility. Phrases such as " . . . in the near future," "it is necessary to resolve this problem shortly," and "let me hear from you regarding this matter," do not box in an opponent. Instead, flexibility is promoted and exchange is solicited. The flexible deadline serves to put the recipient on notice of the existence of the problem and establishes the need for a response without setting a rigid time limit.

The flexible deadline is especially useful in situations that require diplomacy or in those instances where you are not sure you have all the facts and want to engage in a dialogue with your opponent.

It's important to delineate between those situations truly requiring a reticent uncompromising approach and those in which flexibility should be exhibited. You must be cautious not to take inflexible deadline positions continually without documenting your threat and following through if the deadline is not met. Otherwise, you stand to lose all credibility. Flexible deadlines are useful ploys to help you position your case without drawing a hard and fast line. They are a moderate alternative to short-fuse deadline demands.

DEMANDING A PREMIUM FOR IMMEDIATE SATISFACTION

Many cases are settled because of an absence of supporting facts or documentation, lack of provable damages, unfavorable case law, or poor jury verdict expectancy. Another factor to consider in settlement negotiations is the acuteness of the client's immediate needs. "How soon must your client close the deal?" "Is the opposing party under serious time or financial pressures to settle?" "Can your client afford to outwait the opposition?" In many situations involving corporations, financial institutions, and insurance companies, paying a premium for immediate satisfaction becomes a business decision in which the time value of money becomes an overriding factor. Settlements often revolve around the reality that a dollar paid or received today will not carry the same value next month or next year. Consequently, settlement decisions are often tied to sheer dollar-and-cents pragmatics with legal considerations playing a secondary role. This is simply one more application of demanding a premium for immediate satisfaction.

I CAN'T WAIT—SETTLE NOW!

Litigating a lawsuit from beginning to end is a long, arduous task for both attorney and client. The legal system offers defendants numerous places to hide within its complex machinery. Even if the plaintiff is fortunate enough to overcome the many hurdles raised by the defense, the prospect of an appeal still looms. Protracted litigation is expensive and time consuming. The potential rewards for the plaintiff must outweigh these downside considerations. Even if the client is willing to assume the risk of a court fight, he must also be capable of going the distance. Most are not. This is why demanding a premium for immediate satisfaction is a frequently used and often successful settlement ploy.

The success of this tactic rests on the fact that most clients are impatient. They don't understand the legal system and are astounded by how long it takes for a case to be adjudicated fully. Clients usually want their lawyers to wave a magic wand and extract immediate satisfaction measured in dollars. In reality, this seldom happens. Exploiting this common phenomenon is the essence of demanding a premium for immediate satisfaction. As alluded to earlier, while we have discussed this ploy in the context of lawsuit negotiation, it is equally applicable to business transactions.

TAKING THE EASY WAY OUT

By recognizing the needs of the opposition, you can structure settlement offers to give immediate satisfaction in return for a premium concession. Consider the following example:

Lawyer Right represents a client who has a case that is potentially worth $100,000. The defense attorney does not share the plaintiff's assessment as to the value of the case. The only way Lawyer Right and his client will find out if their case is truly worth $100,000 is to litigate.

Lawyer Right is confident and excited about moving the case forward. He is motivated by the professional challenge of litigation and the prospect of a substantial recovery even though it will probably be several years in materializing.

Lawyer Right's client is in a different situation. The psychological pressure caused by the uncertainty of the legal process causes him great concern. The truth is, Lawyer Right's client is scared to death that years of litigation may result in a recovery of zero. To make matters worse, the client needs money now. He wants and needs tangible results as soon as possible.

Lawyer Right's opponent is Lawyer Slow, a cagey old defense lawyer wise in the ways of human nature and of the litigation process. Slow assures Lawyer Right that there will be a long, drawn-out fight with appeals at every level if necessary. But, if Lawyer Right's client would be willing to accept a much lower settlement amount to avoid the hazards of litigation, then maybe "something could be worked out."

A question frequently raised in negotiations between lawyers and their clients now confronts Lawyer Right and his client: "Will you accept a fixed sum certain today even though it will be substantially lower than what you might recover sometime in the future?" In short, "Will you pay a premium for immediate satisfaction of your present needs?"

In the overwhelming majority of cases, clients prefer to control their destiny and thus opt for certainty over uncertainty. Premiums are thus paid to satisfy their immediate financial needs. The lower settlement amount eliminates their psychological concerns. The plaintiff trades the certainty of a reduced settlement for the uncertainty of litigation.

A client's or opponent's demand for immediate satisfaction is analogous to a discount factor. If the potential value of a case is $10,000, the only way the plaintiff will possibly recover that amount is to jump through the seemingly endless hoops of the legal system. To avoid this unpleasant and time-consuming experience, the potential value of the case is discounted.

This scenario is played out daily. It is based on an exploitation of plaintiff's lack of willingness and capability to persevere and press on into the perilous and uncertain future.

HOW TO APPLY THE SAME PLOY TO BUSINESS NEGOTIATIONS

Immediate satisfaction is often used in business negotiations. Transactions involving cash down payments and long-term financing are prime examples. The purchase price is often discounted in return for a larger cash down payment. Regardless of the strength of the collateral securing a long-term purchase agreement, there is always a chance of problems arising. In other words, uncertainty. Cash paid today is certain. It satisfies immediate needs and alleviates uncertainty. This is simply another application of paying a premium for immediate satisfaction.

Practice tip: When you are in a position to give the other party immediate satisfaction, be sure to extract a premium in return.

HOW TO USE SURPRISE AS AN EFFECTIVE NEGOTIATING TACTIC

In the legal profession, surprises are something attorneys attempt to guard against. Very rarely is a surprise viewed as something positive.

Accordingly, attorneys invest hours of preparation time prior to a negotiation or trial to eliminate surprises. Unfortunately, no matter how thoroughly an attorney prepares, surprises will still surface from time to time. When surprises do occur and you are fortunate enough to be in a position to take advantage of an unexpected turn of events, don't hesitate to do so.

SURPRISE: THE OFFENSIVE PERSPECTIVE

When a startling bit of information presents itself, the natural urge is to use it immediately in hope of securing a quick knockout punch. In actuality, this result rarely occurs. It's more likely that the announcement of some surprising news will be brushed aside by the opposition as inconsequential, equalized in short order, or simply ignored. Instead of squandering surprise information on unproductive dramatics, it should be used as a catalyst or tool to advance and develop an existing strategy or tactic. When used in a deliberate fashion, surprise information serves to accelerate you toward your objective.

For example, assume you are engaged in a negotiation with another attorney over a question of whether a contract between your respective clients is enforceable. Your opponent confidently recites all the reasons why your client will be held responsible if the case proceeds to trial. His objective, of course, is to increase your uncertainty and thus increase the settlement value of his case. Your adversary's approach is correct in all respects, except for his failure to uncover vital information in the form of a recently decided State Supreme Court case that substantially weakens his legal position. The natural temptation is to interrupt him and say, "I suggest you review the recently decided XYZ case. After you read it, you'll see that your position has no merit." However, there is a better approach.

Let your opponent tell you all the reasons why his client should recover. Hear him out. After he has revealed his entire case, attempt to subordinate all other arguments to case law. Force the opposing attorney to adopt case law as the primary basis for his demands. After he has concluded current case law that supports his position, inject some uncertainty. "Well, I think what you're saying would probably be right under the old line of cases, but didn't the Supreme Court change all that in a recent decision? Let me check on it and I'll be back in touch." You can be sure your opponent will read the case within the hour and learn the unfortunate news for himself. After a few days, you can follow with a letter stating that "in view of the recent Supreme Court ruling in the XYZ case, we feel your previous position will by necessity be subject to reappraisal. Nonetheless, we will be glad to work with you to resolve this matter in short order. To do so, we propose the following action...."

Caution: Surprises can backfire. Never lose sight of your objective, the permanent resolution of your client's problem. The key word is permanent. Surprises hurled at an opponent may give you a temporary, short-term advantage; however, in the long run, using surprise against an opponent will create distrust, impair communication, and motivate him to prolong the dispute to save face even if he has little chance of ultimate success. Nobody likes to have a smug opponent point out shortcomings, errors, and weaknesses. It's not smart negotiation.

To avoid these problems and still derive permanent maximum benefits, help your opponent arrive at the inescapable conclusion initiated by your surprise information. The effect will be less dramatic but much more profitable for your client.

SURPRISE: THE DEFENSIVE PERSPECTIVE

Unwanted surprises can manifest themselves in a number of ways. New demands, presentation of new issues, shortened deadlines, irrational arguments, or the discovery of shocking information damaging to your client's position are the most common examples. As stated earlier, even though a negotiator prepares thoroughly, he is still subject to the unexpected. Delay is the key to fending off an opponent's use of surprise. Any maneuver designed to buy time will help soften the impact of surprise. In most cases, once you have gained enough time to analyze and adjust to the new information, you can cope with most surprises by taking steps to neutralize the short-term advantage gained by the opposition.

PATIENCE: ONE OF THE MOST POWERFUL WEAPONS IN THE NEGOTIATOR'S ARSENAL

Americans by their nature are impatient. The prevailing attitude is "Let's get the show on the road—now!" This national character trait has a direct bearing on American attorneys in the way they negotiate with one another and with lawyers from other countries. Typically, American attorneys are viewed by their counterparts in other countries as always being impatient. Conversely, Americans tend to view most foreign lawyers as being lackadaisical, with little concern for getting immediate results. As a general rule, it is difficult for American negotiators to demonstrate patience unless they have been through many bargaining sessions. Patience is a learned virtue. It develops with maturity and experience.

Patience is one of the most powerful ploys in the negotiator's arsenal. Potentially, it is the ultimate ploy. The negotiator who develops the ability to absorb tension without submitting to the pressures of premature settlement is an adversary to be respected. The exercise of patience can rob the opposition of his superiority in facts, law, and leverage.

The advantages that flow from using patience as a ploy are grounded in the leverage of timing. The patient negotiator is always in a position to maximize timing opportunities throughout a negotiation. Patience leads to:

- Concessions
- Reducing an opponent's expectation level
- Discovery of new alternatives
- Desirable settlements

When two equally matched negotiators enter into bargaining, the one exhibiting the most patience will usually prevail.

Practice tip: As a general rule, quick settlements that prove unsatisfactory are usually the result of poor judgment and lack of patience on the part of one of the negotiators.

AFFIRMATIVE INACTION:
WHEN THE BEST MOVE IS NO MOVE

Periodically, you will find yourself in situations where the best move is no move. That is, simply do nothing. We refer to the ploys used in these situations as "Affirmative Inaction." There are four basic types of Affirmative Inaction.

- Going silent
- Ground zero—your move
- Let the situation deteriorate
- Collapse

WHEN GOING SILENT CAN BE EFFECTIVE

Lawyers love to talk. As a group, they find it difficult to control their urge to speak up even in situations where communication is damaging. The skilled negotiator, however, is the exception to the rule. He knows when and why to go silent.

There are two primary instances when silence can be used as an active negotiating ploy.

EXPAND YOUR KNOWLEDGE BASE

Consider the situation where you do not have all the facts. You know that due to missing information your grasp of the case is fuzzy and uncertain. Silence can be used as an affirmative inaction ploy to increase your knowledge base. By soliciting information from your opponent and encouraging him to talk, your silence will permit the opposition to disclose vital aspects about the negotiation. Chances are your opponent will reveal more information than he needs to. So much the better for you.

SILENCE AND DEPOSITIONS

Silence is used as a ploy to gain information from opposing parties and witnesses at depositions. The trick is to construct short, direct questions to the witness and then back off, letting the witness ramble. The less interruption the better. The witness feels he is carrying the conversation and therefore must say something to keep the discussion alive. The result is a successful deposition with a transcript filled with pages of testimony for the witness, not questions from the attorney. To achieve this result, you must consciously suppress your desire to engage in argument or dialogue. Go silent and let the witness do the talking.

SILENCE AS A SHIELD

In situations where the opposition is engaged in a verbal blitzkrieg against you, simply go silent. Silence neutralizes this type of opponent quickly. Your opponent will soon run out of steam, especially if he is failing to get a reaction from you. His staccato pace cannot be maintained without resting points that are supplied when you intervene with a response. Remain silent and let your opponent wear himself out.

SILENCE HELPS YOU PLAY IT CLOSE TO THE VEST

Silence is an excellent ploy for restricting the amount of information you want passed to the other side. This is especially true in situations where you are attempting to camouflage a weak position. Silence helps you disguise the soft spots. By limiting the amount of information you broadcast to the other side, you decrease the chance of the opponent discovering and exploiting your weaknesses.

SILENCE IS NOT AVOIDANCE

Don't confuse silence with avoidance. Silence is affirmative inaction. There should always be a reason for your failure to speak or act. An experienced negotiator using silence as a ploy will outwardly appear to be open and will likely be very accommodating when a request is made to hold a meeting or to engage in a telephone conversation. The reason will most likely be that your opponent wants information from you. To achieve this result, he will put the burden of carrying the discussion squarely on you while he simply sits back and listens. If you are on the wrong side of a one-way conversation, beware.

Practice tip: Silence is like a magnet. It attracts information without divulging any in return. When you go silent, know why and make a point to listen.

GROUND ZERO—YOUR MOVE

This ploy rests on the basic fact that all cases start at ground zero. To move past this point, the plaintiff's attorney must take action. The first step may be a phone call, a demand letter, lawsuit, or some other initiative. In most situations, the defense attorney is in an excellent position to use the "Ground Zero—Your Move" ploy. Unless the opposition makes a move, the case stays at ground zero. Your ploy is simply to do nothing until the other side moves from ground zero. Each time the opposition moves the case (e.g., filing a lawsuit), you can return it to ground zero with a balancing move (e.g., filing an answer). The next move is your opponent's.

USING THE GROUND ZERO—YOUR MOVE PLOY

A good example of the ground zero ploy at work is an insurance defense lawyer who is threatened with a lawsuit. The parties start at ground zero. The initial and most cost-effective ploy by the defense lawyer is simply to do nothing. Unless suit is actually filed, nothing more will be required. Often, the lawsuit never comes. Money never changes hands on the strength of empty threats. In our example, it was up to the plaintiff's attorney to press the claim and move the case off ground zero. He never did. The defendant wins.

LET THE SITUATION DETERIORATE

Sometimes your position is improved when the situation gets worse. For instance, consider the plight of a minority stockholder who has attempted to get corporate management to hold annual stockholder meetings but to no avail. Notice of demand to hold annual meetings is sent to corporate management but still no action is taken. In addition, notice of demand to furnish the minority stockholder financial statements is also ignored by corporate management. With each refusal, the minority shareholder believes that his situation looks more bleak—or does it? To the contrary, as the situation gets worse the minority stockholder's case gets stronger. The consistent and obstinate refusal on the part of corporate management to afford the minority shareholder his basic rights under the corporate bylaws will ultimately cement the stockholder's legal position and be the undoing of management. The case against corporate management was good after the first refusal, better after the second, and even better after the third.

COLLAPSE: WHEN TO AVOID CONFRONTATION AT ALL COSTS

The collapse ploy may be used in situations when you want to avoid battle or confrontation at all costs. Consider the following example:

A small family-owned business finds itself in an unmanageable financial bind. It becomes apparent that the business cannot survive.

The only way to avoid continuing losses, which will ultimately lead to bankruptcy, is to liquidate the business, pay its creditors, and close down. All factors indicate that liquidation is the most desirable alternative under the circumstances, except for one point. Unfortunately, the business has just renewed its lease agreement for another six-year term. To make matters worse, the lease has been guaranteed by personal endorsements of the owners. As attorney for this small business, you are faced with the following points to consider:

- Client has ruled out bankruptcy as an alternative.
- The new lease agreement is valid and enforceable in all respects.
- Landlord is financially strong and respected in the community.
- Tenant is extremely weak financially.
- Liquidation will barely pay all outstanding debts and other expenses.
- Individual owners have no assets from which to draw funds to make a settlement proposal to the landlord, or to engage in litigation.

Your primary objective is to convince the landlord to rescind the lease agreement voluntarily. Keeping in mind that your client has no money to fund a settlement proposal, or to spend on litigation that he would most likely lose, the consequences are obvious. You are at the landlord's mercy. How do you go about convincing the landlord to voluntarily cancel the lease? The answer: Use the "Collapse" ploy.

The value of Collapse stems from neutralizing the hostility factor present in most lawsuits. Lawsuits are spawned by parties who have antagonized one another. If hostility between the parties is high, lawsuits normally emerge as a natural consequence. Collapse is designed to remove or reduce hostility so that litigation can be avoided and settlement reached. The conversation with the landlord would go something like this:

"My clients are extremely upset about having to close down their business. As you know, they have been in business for over nine years. But in view of the last eighteen months, they have been forced to realize that the business can't continue. They simply must liquidate now before the situation gets completely out of hand. At present, bankruptcy is not an alternative. My clients are fully aware that you have the capability and right to drag them through court over this lease agreement. They certainly have no desire to fight with someone with whom they have had such a good relationship for so long. As embarrassing as it is for my clients, they are asking for your help."

This approach eliminates all hostility even though the tenant is going to have to default on the lease agreement. The attorney fully admits that the landlord has the ability and right to sue his clients. But while admitting these points, he asks for help. It's very difficult for hostility to emerge between two parties when one party is sincerely asking for help. Collapse is a request to the opposition to show mercy. It's much easier for a strong opponent to rationalize leniency if he generally likes the person requesting help.

Practice tip: Lawsuits are normally spawned by parties who have antagonized one another to the point of open hostility. Collapse attempts to eliminate the hostility factor and avoid litigation.

DEMANDS: A KEY TO UNDERSTANDING THE NEGOTIATING PROCESS

Everyone is subject to demands, especially lawyers. Letters, phone calls, and lawsuits are all vehicles for the countless demands and counterdemands that are a natural part of any lawyer's practice. Demands can range in extremes from outrageous ultimatums to fair requests to empty bluffs. Formulating and reacting to demands comprises much of a lawyer's practice. Because the substance and manner in which a demand is made can have a pronounced effect on a negotiation, it is important that you develop an appreciation and understanding of demands.

THE DEMAND PATTERN FORMULA: NO–WHY?–TOO HIGH

The initial reaction to most demands in legal negotiation is "No." As time passes and the negotiators exchange information and develop a working relationship, the "No" response usually mellows to a "Why?"—why do you think that your demand is fair? Why do you need that particular point? Eventually, "Why?" turns to "Too high"—you're asking for too much. So the typical response pattern to demands is "No—Why?—Too High." If you are the negotiator issuing the demand, your response to counterproposals generally will follow the same pattern: "No—Why?—Too Low."

As negotiations proceed, this pattern is repeated until the gap separating the negotiators is finally bridged. If the gap is not closed by negotiation, a business deal never materializes or in the case of a legal claim, litigation ensues.

USING CREDIBLE UNCERTAINTY TO BRIDGE THE GAP

When it comes time to make a demand, most attorneys fall into a common trap. They either structure their demands unrealistically high, making substantive negotiation impossible or unfeasible; or they make the demand too low, thereby seriously devaluing their case. In both instances, their demands lose impact. Neither excess creates credible uncertainty in the mind of the opposition. Before we look at how to use credible uncertainty in structuring demands, let's first examine these two traps in more detail.

SHOOT FOR THE MOON

This trap is characterized by the view that if you don't ask for it, you'll never get it. This occurs when one side makes a ridiculous demand that will almost always be viewed by the opposition as absurd. Even though chances are slim that such an offer will ever be effective, many negotiators try it on the off chance that it might work. Their reasoning is simple: You never know till you ask. The worst the other side can do is say no. We can always lower our sights later. As a result, shooting for the moon is a frequently used tactic.

LEAVING MONEY ON THE TABLE

Conversely, when your demand is too low, you run the risk of having the offer snapped up, leaving money on the table. On the other hand, if the offer is not taken seriously, you jeopardize the final settlement amount. When this happens, the opposition will perceive your position as one of weakness. A low initial demand will quickly devalue your case in the eyes of your opponent. As happens in the Shoot for the Moon Trap, the low demand fails to create any uncertainty. As a result, it does not receive serious consideration.

CREDIBLE UNCERTAINTY:
THE KEY TO MAKING EFFECTIVE DEMANDS

The key to making good demands is to maintain a balance between shooting for the moon and leaving money on the table. You want to make a demand that will invoke maximum credible uncertainty. For example, assume you have been retained to represent a client who has been injured in a minor automobile accident. Assume you have concluded that a fair settlement amount is $5000. However, if the case goes to trial, you have determined that potential jury verdict expectancy would be in the $10,000 to $12,000 range. What should your opening demand be?

If you demand $100,000, would this invoke uncertainty in the mind of the opposition? No. The defense attorney has access to the same jury verdict expectancy charts. He knows that his maximum exposure is only $12,000 if in fact you push the case to trial. Your $100,000 would be ignored.

On the other hand, assume you offer to settle the case for $1000. Such demand would indicate to your opponent that you don't know the value of your case and probably don't know what you're doing. He'll either try to snap it up or ignore it. In either event, you lose.

HOW TO CREATE CREDIBLE UNCERTAINTY

However, consider making a demand of $8750. This amount invokes credible uncertainty on the opposition. They are compelled to consider your demand. Because the demand is lower than the probable jury verdict, the defense must determine if its case is strong enough to avoid a jury verdict higher than the settlement offer. The defense has a decision to make. Though they will likely make a counteroffer, the negotiation process has begun. The parties' respective positions begin to narrow as a result of the credible certainty of the plaintiff demand.

BOOST YOUR OFFER FOR LATER CONCESSIONS

Once you determine your optimum range for provoking credible uncertainty on the opposition, add an additional amount to be used as trade points. You know from the demand pattern that regardless of the amount of your first demand, the response from the opposition will almost always be negative. When you reach stage two and your opponent is asking why you think the amount demanded is fair, you will be in a credible position to tell him.

To calculate a demand that will create credible uncertainty, you must first consider proof problems, applicable law, and jury verdict expectancy. All of these elements help you substantiate why your demand is fair. When you reach stage three of the demand pattern—Too High—the extra amount you added at the outset provides you with trade points that you can concede to the opposition without discounting the true value of your claim.

The demand–counterdemand pattern will continue back and forth with each side adjusting its demand up or down depending on the circumstances affecting the case. By carefully considering the amount of your initial demand and formulating it on fact rather than wishful thinking, you will put yourself in a much better position to play this game successfully.

Practice tip: Structure your demands to expose your opponents to maximum credible uncertainty.

BEWARE OF BRACKETING

You should always be aware that each demand or counterdemand acts to constrain the negotiators. We refer to this as *bracketing*. This is the principle behind the floor/ceiling trap previously discussed. To illustrate: Assume you originally offer to settle a case for $25,000. The opposition counters with $2000; you counteroffer $15,000. The negotiation is now confined to the $15,000 to $2000 range. In this instance, the brackets have worked in favor of the negotiator making the $2000 offer of settlement. Why? This negotiator's exposure has been reduced from $25,000 to $15,000 for a mere $2000 in return. The defense lawyer has reduced his uncertainty level at the equivalent rate of twenty cents on the dollar. Not bad.

DON'T GET ROPED IN

Bracketing can work to the benefit of both sides in that it helps narrow the issues and amount in controversy. But beware that you do not become trapped within too small an area. This situation frequently occurs in negotiations between insurance adjusters and attorneys where the primary issue generally comes down to money. Normally in this type of settlement negotiation, the plaintiff's counsel will submit an itemization of all medical expenses and other damages in support of his total demand. The initial reaction from the adjuster is one of shock (the "No" phase of the demand pattern). After the typical exchange of information and explanation of certain facts, the "Why?" phase of the demand pattern is completed. Next comes the attempt to bracket-in the attorney. The adjuster may say, "Let's see if we can settle this case. How much do you really think it's worth? Give me a fair demand and I'll see what I can do to dispose of this file." Beware, the tendency is to be fair, just, and reasonable and say, "Well, we would be willing to take X amount." At this point, you have been bracketed between the amount the insurance company previously offered and your quotation. The case will not settle at your fair and reasonable amount. Instead, negotiations will continue in an attempt to reduce the actual amount even farther below your settlement target.

To understand fully the implications of the adjuster knowing your actual assessment of the claim's value, consider the reverse. What if you as a plaintiff's attorney could ask the same question of the insurance adjuster and get an answer. "Well, after much thought, the company thinks the claim is really worth $20,000." Wouldn't this be helpful information from your standpoint as the plaintiff's negotiator?

KEEP YOUR DEMANDS FLEXIBLE

To avoid the pitfall of bracketing, try to keep your demands flexible. For instance, you could respond to an adjuster seeking to bracket you with, "Well, I truly believe our case is worth exactly what I asked for in our initial demand because of the reasons I've already stated. Nonetheless, I would be willing to recommend to my client that we discount this amount in return for an expedited settlement. It's really up to you as to how much we might be willing to discount depending on how long you want to delay settlement of the case."

Even though a settlement range will emerge, the brackets are flexible. The negotiator is still in a good position to seek a settlement without confining himself to a limited settlement area in the event discussions break down.

LIMITED AUTHORITY: THE NEGOTIATOR'S BEST ALLY

The last thing a negotiator wants to do is announce to an opponent that he has full authority to settle a case. A negotiator's best ally is the cloak of limited authority.

THE THREE ADVANTAGES OF LIMITED AUTHORITY

The negotiator vested with limited authority has three distinct advantages over the negotiator empowered with full authority.

LIMITED AUTHORITY: THE NEGOTIATOR'S BACK DOOR

First, limited authority gives you the option to avoid making decisions whenever it suits you. It becomes the negotiator's back door. No matter what kind of predicament you face, you can always defer making a decision until you have had the opportunity to confer with your principal, client, boss, or whomever. How many times have you heard another attorney say, "Let me check with my client and I'll get back to you about your settlement offer"? The ploy of limited authority is used throughout the business world to insulate against spontaneous or reactionary decisions. Insurance adjusters always seem to have to check with their regional supervisor before concluding a settlement; bank loan officers always have to refer a request to the loan committee; corporate officers consult their boards of directors; government officials must seek the approval of their department heads.

Limited authority insulates the negotiator. It's a legitimate out to an aggressive opponent who is pressing for an on-the-spot decision. This can provide a definite advantage when faced with a pressurized situation requiring an immediate decision.

LIMITED AUTHORITY JUSTIFIES A HIGHER AUTHORITY

Limited authority also provides you with the excuse to bring in another negotiator, or a higher authority. For instance, assume you announced at commencement of a negotiation that you have limited authority. Further assume talks reach a standstill several weeks later. In order to move the talks forward, you can inform your opponent that the next session will be attended by the client, senior partner, or whomever in an effort to resolve the problem. This manuever would not be possible had you stated at the outset that the decision to settle was solely up to you.

LIMITED AUTHORITY INSULATES THE REAL DECISION MAKER

Additionally, in cases involving limited authority, the real decision maker is insulated from the heat of the battle. It affords the person making the final decision, usually the client, to do so purely on fact, without becoming swayed by personality or emotional considerations.

While a negotiator never wants to reveal he has full authority, the opposite is true for the opponent. You always want to deal with someone who has full authority. There are two reasons: First, unless you are negotiating with the real decision maker, everything you say in support of your position will be filtered before it reaches the person making the final decision. In essence, you must rely on your opponent to restate your position to his superior. You become dependent on your opponent to sell your case. Needless to say, something will get lost in the translation. Second, by dealing with someone who has limited authority, you are allowing him the same "back door" to evade you when it comes time to make important decisions. Consequently, you never really know where you stand on questions requiring immediate answers. Your opponent is in a position to let the answers linger until it suits him. This is why it is essential to determine who among the opposition has decision-making authority.

Practice tip: Always have a back door to facilitate a quick getaway if needed. Limited authority will provide this back door. Use it.

CONCESSIONS: MAKING A DESIGNED RETREAT

When you engage in a negotiation, you must be prepared to give and take. Demands made during negotiations are the take side of bargaining; concessions are the give side. As we mentioned earlier in this chapter, a timely concession can be just as important as a concession received in concluding a negotiation. Making concessions should not be viewed negatively. Concessions can be used as interim ploys designed to bring you closer to your objective. Some negotiators refer to concession making as "designed retreat."

THE ROLE OF TRADE POINTS

In order to know what you can concede, you must have a plan designating your deal points, secondary points, and trade points. This last category is comprised of your concessions or throwaways. These are points that you intend to give up during the negotiation. They are sometimes referred to as straw men. The key to using trade points depends upon your success in inflating their value before offering them as concessions. The more your opponent believes they are worth, the more he will in turn concede to you.

THE CARDINAL RULE OF MAKING CONCESSIONS

We've mentioned this before, but its importance bears mentioning again. Never make a concession unless you get something in return. Trading concessions is the classic example of the quid pro quo—something for something. Always get something for anything you might give up, regardless of whether it is an insignificant trade point or substantive concession.

NINE POINTS TO FOLLOW WHEN MAKING CONCESSIONS

You should adhere to the following guidelines when making concessions:

- Always build in trade points in your negotiating plan.
- Inflate the value of your trade points.
- Confine your concessions to trade points; avoid concessions on secondary points until late in a negotiation.
- Conserve concessions. One way to increase the value of trade points is to delay conceding them until the eleventh hour.
- Pace your concession rate. Never give up too much, too fast. Make your opponent work for each concession. This will help increase the value of your trade points.

- Be aware of what you are conceding versus what you are receiving.
- Avoid giving away a big chunk. Dole out concessions in little pieces. Again, this increases the value of your giveaways.
- Don't hesitate to take back a concession. Threatened concession redemption often leads to reciprocal concessions from an opponent.
- Avoid making the first concession.

Practice tip: Never make a concession unless you get something in return

PERSUASIVE PLOYS: TWO TECHNIQUES FOR CLOSING THE GAP BETWEEN YOU AND YOUR OPPONENT

As we stated at the beginning of this chapter, the negotiating process is an attempt to persuade the opposition to adopt a new position closer to your own. The various moves you make throughout the bargaining process are designed to entice the opposition to close the gap toward your objective. Consequently, all moves or ploys are by their nature meant to persuade. There are two primary techniques you can use to strengthen the persuasiveness of your ploys.

TECHNIQUES FOR STRENGTHENING YOUR PERSUASIVE PLOYS

Persuasive ploys fall into two categories:

1. Those that project certainty of your position
2. Those that create uncertainty in your opponent's position

PROJECTING THE CERTAINTY OF YOUR POSITION

A technique for promoting certainty is the fair and reasonable man approach. It is based on the premise that you are more likely to persuade an opponent if he views you as being fair and reasonable.

One way to project this image is to substantiate your position at every possible juncture of the negotiation. Provide uncontestable supporting facts, favorable case law, statutory authority, policy considerations, and positive public sentiment to substantiate your position. Substantiation leads to believability. If your opponent believes what you're telling him, your image as being fair and reasonable is enhanced. When a fair and reasonable person is certain of his position, uncertainty starts eroding the confidence of his bargaining counterpart. Your opponent is placed in the position of being viewed as unreasonable if he doesn't agree with you. No one wants to think of himself as unfair or unreasonable.

The key to projecting certainty is to make the circumstances surrounding your case appear favorable to your position by substantiating and supporting your stand with objectively verifiable facts.

CREATING UNCERTAINTY IN YOUR OPPONENT'S POSITION

Conversely, another approach to strengthening your persuasiveness is to design your moves in such a way as to create uncertainty in the opposition's position. A favorite ploy of skilled negotiators is to attack an opponent at his weakest point. Whether it's an unfavorable case law, lack of statutory authority, absence of documentation or witnesses, select the weakest link and press on. Persistently highlighting an opponent's weakness will create uncertainty in his position. By coupling this uncertainty with a confident posture, you will have exerted the maximum forward movement toward your ultimate negotiating objective.

8

The Role of Correspondence

Correspondence, if used properly, can be a key factor in getting what you want in a negotiation. We have touched briefly on other communication skills in terms of preparation and the opening move. These principles are generally applicable to all other phases of bargaining. This chapter focuses on a specific aspect of communication—correspondence. It discusses principles and ploys that recur frequently in the field of law-related negotiation.

CORRESPONDENCE IS A KEY
TO SUCCESS

Negotiation is by no means limited to oral communication. Correspondence and other types of written communication play a vital role in most if not all negotiations in which lawyers are involved. Letters, memoranda, contract drafts, telegrams, and telexes are all examples of correspondence that are used in every phase of the negotiation process, from beginning to end.

THE DISADVANTAGES
OF CORRESPONDENCE

As with the other modes of communication, certain advantages and disadvantages are associated with the use of correspondence. From a negative standpoint, correspondence is impersonal and doesn't lend itself to using emotional appeal. Well-thought-out correspondence takes time and effort to prepare. It tends to slow the pace of a negotiation. For most negotiators, it's simply easier to say what's on your mind than to formulate your thoughts in written form.

THE ADVANTAGES
OF CORRESPONDENCE

The advantages of correspondence are numerous. Correspondence serves to put the opposing party on formal notice. It creates a permanent record of the transaction. It is a powerful device for emphasizing or downplaying certain facts and positions. Correspondence is aptly designed for establishing timeframes and imposing deadlines. Often, tremendous pressure can be exerted on your opponent through correspondence copy power. Correspondence is a very succinct and efficient way to deliver instructions, advise of forthcoming sanctions, and focus the attention of the opposing negotiator on a desired agenda. Well-prepared correspondence is a vital aspect of the bargaining process that can be used to sway the flow of a negotiation without emotionally upsetting your opponent.

A NINE-POINT PLAN
FOR WRITING MORE POWERFUL
DEMAND LETTERS

The skillful use of correspondence in a negotiation can be illustrated by the demand letter. All attorneys write demand letters. Frequently, the preparation of a demand letter is viewed as a perfunctory task. However, when the draftsperson gives his demand correspondence attention, it can indeed become a powerful negotiating weapon.

The negotiator preparing a demand letter should consider the following nine points in his drafting:

1. Give proof positive notice.
2. Educate the recipient as to the facts.
3. Highlight favorable facts.
4. Minimize damaging facts.
5. Control the mood to suit your approach.
6. Focus on the problem.
7. Establish a time frame for action.
8. Advise of sanctions for inaction.
9. Exert pressure through copy power.

GIVE PROOF POSITIVE NOTICE

Correspondence provides you with the opportunity to identify yourself, your client, and the capacity in which you are acting. The identification of your client and authority to act on his behalf are very important procedural points in certain types of legal disputes. Consider a standard opening such as:

"Please be advised that our firm has been retained by Spring Ridge Nursery, Inc., of Houston, Texas, and its president, Mr. J. H. Oakes, has authorized us to contact you regarding...."

Often the mere arrival of a demand letter prepared by an attorney will bring an air of seriousness to a dispute that didn't exist before counsel became involved. Most people, including lawyers, become uneasy when they find an unexpected piece of correspondence in their mail box bearing the return address of an attorney.

To ensure that your demand letter hits the target, be sure it is sent certified mail, return receipt requested. This takes care of the old excuse "I never received that letter." It is also another way to increase the impact of your letter and establish proof positive notice of its acceptance by the recipient.

In addition, be sure to designate your demand letter as certified mail, return receipt requested on the inside address as well as the mailing envelope. By doing so, you will add a sense of formality and urgency to your letter. Consequently, the recipient is likely to be more concerned about its content.

EDUCATE THE RECIPIENT AS TO THE FACTS

Correspondence can serve an excellent instructional function in explaining your client's point of view or his versions of the facts of a particular case without interruption or digression. A well-written demand letter should set forth the basis of your client's claim in a logical and organized manner in language calculated to promote favorable results.

A primary objective of your demand letter should be to convince the other side of the reasonableness and accuracy of the facts presented so as to compel favorable action by the reader. By presenting the facts in a reasonable and even-handed manner, you will be attempting to lead the other side to one inescapable conclusion—to act in accordance with the request made in the letter.

Several key phrases can help accomplish this objective. For instance, beginning the fact presentation paragraph of your letter with "According to our client..." serves to show the other side you recognize that his interpretation of the facts may be different. By acknowledging that the facts presented in your letter represent the plaintiff's viewpoint, communication and open exchange with the opposition is promoted.

Practice tip: As any experienced attorney knows, clients tell their attorney what they want them to know or what they think they want to hear. Consequently, it's dangerous to think you know the whole story after you have heard only one version of the facts. Don't box yourself in by blindly accepting your client's version of the facts. Leave yourself room for maneuvering in case your client's version of the story isn't totally accurate. "According to our client" will help do just that.

To further promote open exchange of communication with the other side, prevent misunderstandings, and put your opponent in a position of having to respond, insert the following phrase: "However, if our client is not aware of all the facts surrounding this matter, please advise us accordingly care of this office." It helps to follow with, "In the event we do not hear from you on or before (a short-fuse deadline date), we must assume the facts related by our client are accurate and complete."

HIGHLIGHT FAVORABLE FACTS

One of the advantages of preparing correspondence is that you are in a position to formulate the letter to accent your client's position favorably. If, for instance, the facts tend to lean in your direction, highlight those facts. If, on the other hand, the law is in your favor, talk about the legal aspects of the case. Regardless of your strong-point, highlight and magnify it in your demand letter.

MINIMIZE DAMAGING FACTS

Conversely, correspondence is an excellent way to downplay damaging facts. There is no requirement that you draw attention to or highlight the negative aspects of your client's case. The structure of your letter, word selection, and the presence or omission of certain points can help you devalue and deemphasize the negative aspects of your client's case. Your objective is to convince the opposition that your client has no weak points. Sometimes that objective is best served by simply steering away from disputed facts, if possible.

CONTROL THE MOOD TO SUIT YOUR APPROACH

A derivative advantage of highlighting strong points and minimizing weak ones is the ability to control the mood and tone of your approach with the opposition. For example, assume you receive a letter from the other side blasting your client and raising several new issues that you consider to be irrelevant to the case. The tendency is to fire back with a strongly-worded rejoinder of your own. The danger of this approach is an escalation of harsh feelings and polarized positions, or even a breakoff of talks. Normally, this is the one consequence you want to avoid. It will usually be in your client's best interest to maintain a dialogue with the other side. You can use correspondence to regulate the tone of your response so as to accomplish this purpose. For instance, your response could begin with "This will acknowledge and thank you for your letter of..." From this point on, pick and choose the topics you wish to address in a nonemotional, businesslike manner. The necessary conciliatory mood was created in the first sentence. The remainder of the letter should be drafted to support this tone throughout.

FOCUS ON THE PROBLEM

Always keep correspondence focused on the real problem. Conversely, good strategy for situations in which the law and facts are both against you is to "muddy the water" or confuse and entangle issues to a point where the real problem becomes camouflaged and sometimes lost. Correspondence can keep you and your opponent on or off track as the situation warrants.

Practice tip: A good time to use correspondence to focus on desired topics is immediately following a meeting or telephone conversation in which a plethora of unrelated collateral issues may have been injected in the discussion. A letter sent to your opponent immediately after the discussion omitting all the unrelated topics and emphasizing the ones of importance to you serves to keep the negotiators focused on the real topics of concern to you.

ESTABLISH A TIMEFRAME FOR ACTION

One of the most important aspects of any demand letter is to motivate the other side to act: to do something, or refrain from doing something. A principle component in achieving this result is establishing a time frame in which you expect the other side to act. Correspondence is an excellent way of imposing a deadline on an opponent.

When a deadline is imposed orally, there is margin for misinterpretation: "I thought you said April 21 not April 1" or "I don't remember you ever saying anything about a deadline." However, when the deadline is imposed by the letter, especially when it is a confirmation of a deadline already imposed in previous discussion, there is no room for error. Imposing your deadline by letter tends to make the other side accept the time frame as authentic. The permanence of a writing also tends to underscore and give added emphasis to the deadline data.

ADVISE OF SANCTIONS FOR INACTION

You've heard the expression "Ignorance is bliss." It's especially true within the context of negotiation. Often when dealing with nonlawyers, unless you state specific sanctions that could be imposed for inaction, the opposing party may have no idea of the consequences. Consequently, it's important for you to educate the opposition as to their potential exposure and liability.

An effective way of making the opposition aware of potential negative repercussions is to suggest the course of action you intend to pursue should the opposition fail to take the action requested in your letter.

For instance, the following phrase could be used: "In the event we do not hear from you on or before the above date, we will have no other alternative but to institute appropriate legal proceedings. If such action becomes necessary, we will request the court to grant us attorney's fees, pre- and post-judgment interest, and all costs of court in addition to the principal amount demanded herein."

Practice tip: Once your opponent realizes that his failure to meet your demands may result in far greater costs in the future, there is a greater likelihood of compelling him to act in your favor. The key is making your opponent aware of what could happen if he doesn't meet your demands.

EXERT PRESSURE THROUGH COPY POWER

Demand correspondence should not necessarily be confined just to the sender and the receiver. The demand letter can be further strengthened by involving other parties in the written communication. We refer to this ploy as "Copy Power."

Everyone has a superior or watchdog of some kind. Officers of large public corporations have directors, shareholders, and government regulatory agencies. Employees have employers. Attorneys have their clients, judges, and fellow attorneys. We are all subject to review and reprimand. Consequently, we all have certain pressure points. You can create leverage by exploiting the opposition's pressure points through Copy Power.

Practice tip: Copy Power is particularly effective when dealing with large organizations and governmental entities. If you want to substantially increase your chances of getting a large corporation or federal agency to act, send a copy of your demand letter to appropriate corporate officials or elected officers. More times than not you will provoke a response or reaction that will help you achieve the desired result.

Despite the pros of Copy Power, there are downside risks as well. There is always the risk of backing your opponent into a corner or alienating those you seek to influence with a copy of your letter. Always think twice before invoking Copy Power.

Consider the following demand letter in which the text has been cross-referenced to the nine points previously discussed.

January 10, 1983

Mr. Paul Chaffey, President   CERTIFIED MAIL
LONDON SMILE PRODUCTIONS, INC.   RETURN RECEIPT
243 Music Square West   REQUESTED
Nashville, Tennessee   (1)

RE: Wrongful Use of Master Recordings and Copyright
    Infringement—CHANTEY MUSIC COMPANY, INC.

Dear Mr. Chaffey:

(1) Please be advised that our law firm has been retained by
Chantey Music Company, Inc., of Los Angeles, California. We have
been authorized by its President to contact you regarding the
unlicensed use of several copyrights and master recordings owned
by it.

(2) According to our client, beginning in March 1955 you entered
into a series of lease agreements with Chantey Music Company,
Inc., wherein the lessors leased to you the rights to certain master
recordings (*see* Exhibit "A"). Concurrently, you were issued a
license to use the copyrighted material as contained on said master
recordings. The term of each lease agreement was eighteen months
with the first agreement expiring in August 1957 and with later
lease agreements expiring as late as 1958. All music licenses granted
you also expired on or before August 1958. The lease agreements
clearly provided that upon termination all masters and mechanical
parts would be returned to the lessor. (5) According to our client
you did not comply with this provision and have willfully and
wrongfully maintained possession of the masters even though
repeated requests have been made for their return.

(3) In 1982, well after the expiration of the last lease agreement, our
client became aware that you had apparently released an album on
the Sundance label entitled "Sam Sings the Blues" (stock no. 5005)
containing two of the recordings that had been previously leased to
you. Such action was in direct contrast to your statements that the
masters could not be returned to our client because they had been
misplaced and were lost.

(2) (4) It appears from the aforementioned facts that you have
wrongfully converted our client's property and infringed its
copyrights. However, if our client is not aware of all the facts
surrounding this matter, please advise us accordingly at the address
herein above. In the event we do not hear from you on or before
January 20, 1983, we must assume the facts as known by our client
are accurate.

(1) (6) In any event, this letter shall serve as NOTICE that you are
to cease and desist from using our client's property. In addition, we
are hereby demanding a full and complete accounting of all records
and/or mechanical parts manufactured, sold, leased, or consigned in
connection with the wrongful use of our client's property along
with an accounting of all advances paid you for any record leases.
Finally, we are demanding immediate return of all masters and
mechanical parts related to our client's property.

(7) (8) In the event we do not hear from you on or before January 20, 1983, or receive the requested accounting and property by the same date, we will have no other alternative but to institute the appropriate legal action in which we will seek the maximum statutory damages allowed for copyright infringement.

Sincerely,

FRASCOGNA & HETHERINGTON

X. M. Frascogna, Jr.

XMFjr/ae
Attachment

(9)cc: Darien Blackmon, Director
London Smile Productions, Inc.

Grey Flasko, Director
London Smile Productions, Inc.

Chuck Ozier, Director
London Smile Productions, Inc.

Ouida S. Shay, Director
London Smile Productions, Inc.

GAINING THE EDGE IN PAPERWORK: THINK BEFORE YOU WRITE

All of the points covered in our discussion on how to write effective demand letters are equally applicable to other forms of correspondence that are used in negotiation. Letters, memoranda, telexes, and draft agreements can be used for much more than just basic communication. Each of the nine points listed previously can be used separately or in conjunction with each other to give you an edge from the standpoint of paperwork. Because so much can be accomplished with well-thought-out correspondence, we urge you to subscribe to this very basic and simple rule: Think before you write.

9

Counterattacking

Many experienced attorneys will tell you that the best defense is a good offense. They're right. Why? Because the key to fending off threats of a lawsuit and shifting the momentum of bargaining in your favor is based on how successful you are at putting your opponent "at risk."

THE "AT RISK" FACTOR UNDERLIES ALL EFFECTIVE COUNTERATTACKS

Every attorney has been in the position of representing an angry client who wanted to sue someone regardless of the chances of recovery. Typically, the case is reviewed and an opinion rendered regarding the feasibility of obtaining a judgment. Even though the outlook is not bright, there are always clients who want the suit filed anyway. However, if the client is alerted to possible counterclaim exposure, the case suddenly takes on a different complexion. The enraged client becomes more subdued and starts analyzing his alternatives in a more rational manner. In many cases, the client is willing to forget about a lawsuit that might expose him to liability. This is the "at risk" concept in action.

As we discussed previously, people are motivated by self-interest. They institute lawsuits only when they believe their self-interest will be served. However, when one's self-interest is placed in jeopardy, or at risk, potential plaintiffs become hesitant about resorting to litigation. This is true, even in situations in which their claim may be meritorious and has a good chance of success. Suing is one thing; being sued is quite another. The effectiveness of all of the counterattacking ploys and techniques dealt with in this chapter hinge on your ability to put your opponent at risk.

141

COUNTERDEMANDS:
HOW THEY WORK

As mentioned in Chapter Seven, everyone is subject to demands. A quick way to reverse the demand pattern is to issue demands of your own. To illustrate the use of counterdemands, consider the following domestic relations case.

The attorney for the husband has tactfully persuaded opposing counsel to make the first settlement proposal. Instead of coming forward with a reasonable offer upon which future discussions can proceed, the wife shoots for the moon. She wants everything and nothing less. The husband's attorney is placed in the position of responding to her preposterous demand. How should he approach his opponent? Should he counter with a reasonable counterdemand, or try to explain why the wife's demands are too high? The husband's attorney does neither. Instead, he makes a counterdemand that is an exact duplicate of the wife's demand, the only difference being that it is the husband who is shooting for the moon. The counterdemand cancels the wife's demand; the case goes back to square one. The wife and her attorney are again put in the situation of having to make a realistic proposal or letting the status quo remain unchanged. The only other alternative is to accept the husband's demand or use it as a basis for negotiation. Once in a while, an inexperienced negotiator will fall into the trap of giving credence to the outrageous offer while abandoning his own exorbitant demands. This does not occur often, but it has happened.

FIGHTING FIRE WITH FIRE

In the previous example, the husband's attorney countered his opponent's demand by matching it with one equally unworthy of consideration. In this context, counterdemands say to an opponent, "If you have the gall to think I'll consider such a ridiculous demand, then I have the gall to ask you to consider the same terms." The lesson is clear. When you are presented with a situation in which a totally unrealistic demand is being made of you, neutralize it with a corresponding counterdemand. Fight fire with fire.

Practice tip: Most demands made by your opponents will not be completely out of line as was the demand in our domestic relations example. Nonetheless, even when confronted with a realistic demand, a counterdemand of your own will put your oponent at risk.

CONCESSIONS ARE NECESSARY

Throughout the bargaining process, each negotiator attempts to obtain something of value from his opponent. In most instances, the objective sought has a measurable monetary value. Concessions wrangled from an opponent are viewed as tactical triumphs as well as substantive gains by lawyer and client alike. Gaining a concession reassures the client that his lawyer is fighting on his behalf. For the lawyer, concessions bolster confidence and move the transaction closer to a final positive resolution.

Unfortunately, in the real world of negotiation, everyone sooner or later will find himself in the undesirable position of having to make concessions. No one likes to make concessions; nonetheless, experienced negotiators know that concessions are necessary to resolve disputes. Concessions, when timely made, are the grease that prime the bargaining pump.

Unfortunately, some shortsighted negotiators view concessions made by opponents as a sign of weakness. To these negotiators, a concession is a red flag that spurs them to demand more and concede less. The result is an ever-increasing list of demands fueled by additional concessions. This creates a vicious cycle of escalation that usually results in collapsed talks and no agreement. Pushing the opponent too far, asking for too much, or making too many demands are characteristic of an overreaching negotiator. One way to counteract an overreaching opponent is the "Vanishing Concession."

THE VANISHING CONCESSION: AN EFFECTIVE METHOD TO COUNTERACT OVERREACHING

The Vanishing Concession is based on the premise that once a concession is extracted from an opponent, harmful consequences will result to the negotiator who extracted the concession as well as to his or her client if that concession must be relinquished. The negative consequences can be psychological as well as monetary. The client tends to view the damage in monetary terms. For the negotiator, relinquishing the spoils of victory is more damaging psychologically. In some instances, the client's confidence in his lawyer can be undermined if the lawyer is forced to give up what the client thought had been won. These effects often provide the impetus to break the cycle of overreaching and shift the momentum of bargaining to the negotiator using this counterattacking ploy. To understand the Vanishing Concession fully, consider the following example.

NOW YOU HAVE IT, NOW YOU DON'T

Craig Brass is a 58-year-old insurance adjuster who has worked in the claims department of a major insurance company for over thirty years. Dale Eager, a young plaintiff's attorney, has recently notified Craig of a claim against the insurance company for injuries sustained by his client, Alisa Spender. The insurance company has admitted responsibility for the liability of its insured. The only question is how much it will pay Dale's client.

During the early stages of the negotiation, the parties jockey for position by making extreme offers and counteroffers designed to narrow the true settlement limits. Craig refuses to offer more than $2000 while Dale remains steadfast in his demand for $35,000. Confidentially, Dale believes his case has a realistic settlement value of $10,000 to $12,000.

After the usual pattern of opening moves between the negotiators, Dale decides to accelerate the bargaining process and sends Craig a copy of the complaint he intends to file if the matter cannot be settled in the near future. Shortly thereafter, Craig announces that he is ready to get down to serious business and wishes to dispose of the case by settlement. In this spirit of fairness and cooperation, Craig offers Dale $7500. Dale considers the offer a major concession since the highest offer previously made by the insurance company was only $2000. Elated by this fortunate turn of events, Dale informs his client of the insurance company's offer. Alisa is also pleased with the offer and with Dale's obvious negotiation skills. Alisa feels good about having retained Dale even though several of her friends recommended that she retain Wayne Hubbard, an older, more experienced attorney, to handle her case. Dale asks Alisa to think about the offer for a few days before a response is made to the insurance company.

Alisa joyfully starts calculating to determine what portion of the $7500 settlement will be hers and, just for fun, fantasizes about how she would spend it. After engaging in her imaginary shopping spree, Alisa concludes that her portion of the settlement is not enough to cover her inflated financial needs. Consequently, she advises Dale to try to get $10,000 instead of $7500 from the insurance company. Spurred on by the insurance company's major concession, Dale tells Alisa he is confident he can squeeze another $2000 or $3000 out of Craig.

Dale informs Craig that Alisa wishes to decline the $7500 offer but that she would be willing to accept $15,000. By making demand for $15,000, Dale assumes Craig will counter with $8500. In Dale's view the ensuing pattern of haggling should result in an agreement somewhere in the $10,000 range.

Instead of engaging in Dale's calculated game of give and take, Craig doesn't make any counteroffer. Craig advises Dale that his regional supervisor has reviewed the file and believes that $7500 is too much to pay for a settlement in this case. Craig tells Dale that he is under direct orders to withdraw the $7500 offer—unless, of course, it is accepted prior to notification of its withdrawal. Since Craig is due to report back to his superior by the end of the day, he agrees to give Dale the rest of the day to make a decision. Craig's final words are "It's up to you, Dale. If your client wants the $7500 settlement, fine. I'll tell my supervisor you accepted the company's offer before I withdrew it. If you don't want to settle today for $7500, then consider the offer withdrawn. That's the best I can do."

To make matters worse, Alisa had miscalculated her portion of the $7500 settlement and has been trying to contact Dale to press for even more than the $10,000 they had discussed. She is confident Dale will have no trouble in getting it. What Dale thought he had won suddenly begins to dissolve. Craig turned the tables on Dale and Alisa with the Vanishing Concession.

YOU GOT ME...OH, BY THE WAY, I'M GOING BANKRUPT

The principle behind the Vanishing Concession is frequently used in debtor-creditor negotiations in which the debtor is attempting to settle an outstanding account with the creditor at a reduced amount in an effort to avoid bankruptcy. If the creditor is adamant and unwilling to agree to some type of realistic liquidation plan, the debtor invokes a modified version of the Vanishing Concession ploy. The exchange usually goes something like this:

Creditor's Attorney: "I'm sorry, but my client is unable to accept your settlement proposal of $5200. Unless full payment is made, I've been instructed to file suit."

Debtor's Attorney: "Well, that's a shame, I was hoping we could avoid such drastic action. My client's in a situation where he must either get help from his creditors or be forced to file a petition with the bankruptcy court. He would like to save everyone from suffering a complete loss on their accounts, but he can't do it without some cooperation."

Assuming that bankruptcy would in fact diminish the creditor's chance of recovery, the $5200 offer starts looking a little better—especially when it starts dissolving. The creditor's attorney knows that if he pushes too hard, the $5200 may vanish completely.

Practice tip: Once a concession has been gained, especially if the negotiator and his client have had to invest substantial amounts of time and resources to get it, the prospect of giving it back can be extremely damaging to the apparent victor; therein lies the strength of the Vanishing Concession.

SUBSTITUTING NEW PLAYERS TO GET STALLED NEGOTIATIONS MOVING AGAIN

From a counterattacking standpoint, limited authority provides you with the ability to change participants whenever the situation dictates. Playing this negotiating card can be valuable when talks have reached a stalemate and breakdown is imminent unless some new factor can be injected into the bargaining. Negotiating from an announced position of limited authority gives you the opportunity to substitute participants when the need arises. The ploy of changing participants is illustrated in the following example.

HOW SUBSTITUTING NEW PLAYERS CAN AVOID CATASTROPHE

Assume you are engaged in a negotiation with a large bank on behalf of your client, Paul Welch. Your objective is to keep the bank from foreclosing on Paul's property and to convince the bank's representative that it would be mutually beneficial to reschedule all of

Paul's loans at a lower interest rate over an extended payout period. Throughout the negotiation, you inform the bank's representative, F. M. Bancshares, that if the bank will agree to your plan, Paul's millionaire father-in-law will voluntarily make a sizable payment in reduction of the principal balance. F. M.'s position is inflexible; bring the loans current or else. Eventually talks break down. F. M. informs you that the bank will start foreclosure proceedings at the end of the week. You decide to do two things: first, substitute negotiators; second, appeal to a higher authority. You convince Paul's father-in-law, who is eager to help, to contact the bank's president for an appointment to discuss Paul's problem. The bank's president is receptive to keeping the talks alive since it appears that F. M.'s hard-line attitude may have alienated Paul and his father-in-law. The president knows that unless Paul's father-in-law steps in to help, the bank will have to foreclose on the property and will be faced with a sizable loss. Since Paul has pledged his business assets as collateral for the loan, foreclosure would effectively put him out of business, drying up his only source of income. Paul would have only one alternative at that point—bankruptcy. However, the introduction of new participants can help break the impasse, enabling the negotiation to continue. The prospect of financial loss for all the parties is substantially lessened.

In the foregoing example, the first set of negotiators could not resolve the problem. Without a new twist, the negotiation would have ended in stalemate, forcing the bank to make its only remaining move—foreclosure. The talks were given new life by substituting new participants who continued the negotiation process on a higher level in terms of decision-making authority and without the past rancor that had characterized the bargaining between the lawyer and bank officer. What seemed like a hopeless situation was transformed into a new negotiation.

THE ULTIMATE THREAT:
WHAT TO DO WHEN ALL ELSE FAILS

Another effective counterattacking ploy is making the ultimate threat. This occurs when all else has failed and you have elected to invoke your ultimate threat to put your opponent in a maximum at-risk situation. This ploy can be delivered in the following three ways.

RAISING THE STAKES

When an impasse has been reached and you have decided you must bring the negotiation to a conclusion, raise the stakes to such a point that your opponent can't stay in the game. For instance, in a hard-fought lawsuit that rests on highly technical points of law, inform your opponent that you've decided to write a trial brief that will become the authority on the point in question. If the opposition is not in a position to match you dollar for dollar and hour for hour in responding to such an extensive document, you may force him to settle on favorable terms because the stakes have become too great for him to stay in the game.

THE ULTIMATUM

Typically, this ploy is used in collective-bargaining talks. Labor's ultimate threat is to tell management to meet the union's demands or a strike will be called. The ultimatum can be a very powerful ploy once it's established as being credible and potentially damaging. It creates pressure that can have the effect of breaking a logjam caused by the reticence of management. Ultimatums are frequently made in legal negotiations. Aside from labor negotiations, the most common is the threat of suit: "Either pay my client or we'll file suit."

WITHDRAWAL

Another ultimate threat counterattacking ploy is withdrawal. This ploy is frequently used in the context of diplomatic negotiations. The object of withdrawal is to put the opposition at risk by threatening to break off negotiations. This ploy is most effective when the status quo is in your favor. For example, assume a superstar professional athlete has issued an ultimatum to his team demanding a substantial pay increase. The team's owner calls the superstar's bluff by refusing to meet his salary demands. By doing so, the owner has taken a calculated risk. Drop your demands or walk. The athlete chooses the latter course of action. He walks right into the inviting alternative of a lucrative motion-picture career. Subsequently, talks resume. At this point the athlete is in a perfect position to put the team's owner at risk by threatening to break off the negotiation. The player's downside risks are minimal because of the alternative of a movie career. The newly created status quo suits him fine. The burden now shifts to the owner. The player's demands are no longer backed by bluffs or empty threats. It will be up to the owner to reverse the new status quo. The threat of withdrawal makes the player's demands seem a great deal more palatable to the club owner.

FIGHTING BACK: COUNTERCLAIMS, CROSS-CLAIMS, AND THIRD-PARTY ACTIONS

Trial lawyers are well aware of the power of counterclaims, cross-claims, and third-party actions. In the context of defense litigation, fighting back is often the most effective at-risk device available to the attorney. If you want to counterattack in the world of litigation, you counterclaim, cross-claim, or institute a third-party action.

THE STORY OF DR. ALLEN

Dr. Allen is a world-renowned petroleum geologist. Early in his career, he worked for a small oil company organized in a foreign tax haven. After six years of productive work for the company, and investing a substantial amount of his own money in the company, he decided to embark on a career as an independent petroleum geologist. Once he had begun building his own company, it became apparent that the minority interest he had acquired in his former company was worth little to him. Company management of his old firm simply ignored Dr. Allen. He was not reelected to serve as a director, nor was he given notice of any shareholder meetings, or afforded the right to participate in the company's shareholder stock option programs. To make matters worse, the company's profit-and-loss position was marginal and deteriorating fast. There was little money for exploration and expansion. As far as Dr. Allen was concerned, his former company's future was bleak. Some months after Dr. Allen had resigned himself to this reality, word reached him that his former company had discovered one of the largest oil fields in the Indian Ocean. Not surprisingly, the entire project had been initiated and developed by Dr. Allen from its inception. The discovery completely changed the company's financial outlook. The marginal balance sheet was replaced by one of unlimited potential.

Despite the role Dr. Allen played in helping the company find such a bonanza, he was still being squeezed out. Regardless of past contributions, he was a minority stockholder with little or no influence.

Dr. Allen made attempts to sell his stock, but because the company was closely held there were few bona fide prospects. Finally, after several months, he was contacted by a representative of an investment group expressing interest in acquiring his shares, if the price was right. Eager to sell, Dr. Allen entered into negotiations with the investment group without the aid of legal counsel.

Within a very short time, a deal was made whereby Dr. Allen agreed to sell all his shares to the investment group for $1 million. Telexes were exchanged by the parties and a confirmation letter was sent to Dr. Allen from the investment group's attorney. The deal was locked up and set for closing in fourteen days. Dr. Allen was pleased that at long last he would finally reap the rewards of his labor and financial investment.

Three days before the actual exchange of stock and money was to take place, an international business newspaper published a story announcing that Dr. Allen's former company was going to be acquired by another company on a one-for-one stock exchange. The acquiring company's stock, which was publicly traded, was trading for $40 per share. What Dr. Allen had sold for $1 million was going to be worth $7 million after the acquisition. Dr. Allen was sick, but what could he do? He had exchanged telexes and approved the trade by a confirmation letter. The deal appeared to be airtight. When Dr. Allen voiced his reluctance about carrying out the trade, he was quickly told by the investment group that "We have a deal. Tender your shares or we'll file suit." Ultimately, suit was filed against Dr. Allen when he refused to conclude the sale.

The attorneys defending Dr. Allen were quick to recognize his dilemma. He had been a victim of insider trading. It appeared that two members of the purchasing investment group were also close friends of one of the directors of Dr. Allen's former company. The main problem was finding a connection between the parties in an attempt to overcome the telexes and the confirmation letter signed by Dr. Allen.

THE $6 MILLION COUNTERATTACK

Realizing that the transaction was probably originated by the inside director, Dr. Allen's attorneys decided to put the investment group at risk by bringing an action against the two members of the investment group for alleged insider trading. In addition, a third-party action was brought against all of the directors of his former company for failure to notify Dr. Allen of the pending acquisition. In the event the court compelled Dr. Allen to tender his shares to the purchaser for $1 million, his suit would seek recovery of his lost profit from the directors of his former company. The inside traders were faced with the possibility of losing everything they might gain if the case against Dr. Allen prevailed. In the end, the suit against Dr. Allen was dropped, thereby freeing him to trade his shares for their full $7 million value. The counteractions used by Dr. Allen's attorney put the opposition at risk to the point of saving Dr. Allen $6 million.

Practice tip: When involved as a defendant in litigation, find a way to put the plaintiff at risk by counterattacking. Depending on the facts of the case, counterclaims, crossclaims and third-party actions will often provide you with the ammunition you will need to put the opposition at risk.

THE AFFIRMATIVE DEFENSE

As plaintiff's lawyers will attest, the affirmative defense is second only to a counterclaim in terms of counterattacking effectiveness. The only thing better than a strong affirmative defense is two or three strong affirmative defenses. They make the case more complicated for the plaintiff to prove. A complicated case becomes harder to win because of the increased number of barriers and potential pitfalls produced by the affirmative defenses. Multiple affirmative defenses make the case harder to explain to a judge or jury.

An experienced trial attorney once remarked, "I just filed an answer to a simple replevin suit. In my answer, I raised fourteen affirmative defenses. After the plaintiff's lawyer reads my answer, he won't know what the suit is about."

CREATING PATTERNED DISORDER

In those situations where the counterclaim alternative is not available, you can use another counterattacking ploy—creating patterned disorder.

SAM KROTEK'S FORTRESS

Sam Krotek is a successful businessman. Unfortunately, however, he is involved in too many projects. As a result of Sam's aggressiveness, his organization is in a constant state of disarray. His business records and organizational structure are in a mess. At least that is the opinion of his lawyer and accountant. Despite this, Sam has no trouble finding what he wants to. The fact is, Sam knows where everything is, and exactly how to retrieve it.

When Sam's attorney advises him to clean up his mess, he just laughs. "Why destroy my fortress? I'm safe inside my disorganization. If my own attorney can't untangle this mess, how can you expect the IRS or some plaintiff's lawyer to do it?"

Sam's attitude may not be prudent for many reasons; however, the truth is, he is right about cloaking himself in disorder. As long as you know the secret to untangling the mess if and when necessary, patterned disorder can be useful as a counterattacking ploy. In essence, it tells the opposition "catch me if you can find me." The at-risk elements emerge in uncertainties associated with the disorganization. For instance, "I don't have any assets"; "I don't own stock in that company"; "You are going to have to go through a lot of trouble to prove that point"; or, "Here are my records—I'm sorry, they're in such a mess."

PATTERNED DISORDER: TURNING A DISADVANTAGE
INTO AN ADVANTAGE

Patterned disorder raises barriers against anyone trying to assault you. While we certainly don't recommend that people consciously create a tangle of disorder, it can be an example of turning a disadvantage into an advantage. Conversely, be aware that patterned disorder can be used effectively against you if you ever have occasion to unsnarl the records of a party defendant who owns controlling interest in more paper corporations and marginal bank accounts than any three *Fortune* 500 companies combined. Almost every lawyer has at least one patterned disorder nightmare to recount. They will attest to the effectiveness of this built-in counterattacking measure

10

The Fallback:
a Systematic
Approach to
Dealing with Setbacks

Lawyers are pessimists by nature. While they may hope for the best, they plan for the worst. An attorney's legal training and experience is geared to anticipating potential problems. This is why lawyers are better equipped than most to handle the inevitable setbacks that are bound to crop up over the course of a typical negotiation. Awareness of proven principles and techniques for dealing with the worst if and when it comes is the best insurance any negotiator can have against disaster. This chapter provides a systematic approach to making the best of a bad situation.

DON'T FALL VICTIM TO THE FATAL ASSUMPTION THAT NEGOTIATION MUST RESULT IN AGREEMENT

This is by far the worst mistake any negotiator can make. Despite this fact, people have been dealing themselves undue misery and disappointment for centuries because of their steadfast devotion to this erroneous assumption. Those who fall victim to this fatal assumption equate a successful negotiation with reaching an agreement, any agreement. Members of the "Agreement at All Cost" Club tend to lose sight of just why they are negotiating in the first place. Ostensibly, it's to improve the status quo. However, once the ultimate goal shifts to merely reaching an agreement, substantive negotiating objectives will likely take a back seat to the new priority of closing the deal. When this happens, the seeds of disaster are sown.

I HAVE TO DO SOMETHING, EVEN IF IT'S WRONG

How many times have you heard these familiar words uttered in crisis situations? Probably all too often, even in spite of the futility of such action. This is not to suggest that freezing up and doing nothing is the best way to confront a crisis. When you are in desperate straits, you indeed "have to do something." But how logical is it to take action you know will prove ineffective or even counterproductive? This seemingly obvious bit of common sense should carry over to every crisis negotiation. Unfortunately, it doesn't.

Practice tip: Whenever you are convinced that a negotiated agreement can't or won't accomplish your objectives, you should admit that you are wasting your time. This is your cue to seek alternative solutions. Even if none are readily available, it doesn't make sense to seek an agreement that will leave you in worse shape than you were previously. You would be much better advised to work in the garden or play golf. At least you would have the comfort of knowing you weren't actively making things any worse. In most cases, the status quo can hold its own without you.

HOW TO GAIN AN INSTANT
NEGOTIATING ADVANTAGE OVER YOUR OPPONENTS

Overcoming the deeply ingrained notion that a negotiation must produce an agreement is the key to developing an effective Fallback Strategy. Recognizing that your success doesn't necessarily ride on your ability to forge some type of agreement will provide you with an instant and significant advantage over your opponents, especially those who remain committed to an agreement at all costs. Refusing to be constrained by having to make a deal allows you to be bolder and more confident in your conduct in a given negotiation. This approach also forces you to come to grips with your alternatives. By doing this, you will have effectively constructed a safety net under the negotiation to cushion the blow of failing to reach agreement. That same safety net is not available to the opponent who feels he has no alternative to reaching a negotiated agreement.

HOW TO FORMULATE A WORKABLE
WALK-AWAY POSITION

The Walk-Away Position is the centerpiece to any effective Fallback Strategy. It is simply a predetermined alternative plan of action that can be activated at any point you determine that a negotiated agreement would be counterproductive. The first step in formulating your Walk-Away Position involves an ongoing assessment of your objectives, leverage, and the circumstances surrounding the negotiation. This is crucial to drawing the line between productivity and counterproductivity. When doing this, keep in mind that your assessment can and probably will fluctuate as circumstances change, time elapses, and strengths and weaknesses of the parties are revealed. The key is to remain realistic and flexible while constantly reassessing prospects for reaching a conclusion that will coincide with your objectives.

IDENTIFY YOUR ALTERNATIVES

The next step to formulating your Walk-Away Position is to identify your alternatives to an agreement. If you are going to walk away, it's essential that you know not only what you're walking away from, but also the alternative that you are moving toward. This is essential to making the Walk-Away Position work for you. It may turn out that you have few, if any, alternatives to a negotiated agreement. If this is the case, you will have to make some hard choices that might include making a greater commitment to a negotiated agreement. However, at the very least, you will have to come to terms with the worst possible scenario before it actually presents itself. When and if the worst comes, you will be in a position to elect the best available option under the circumstances. This is always preferable to being forced to cling to a deal that will only worsen your own relative position.

THE WALK-AWAY POSITION
IN ACTION

To illustrate the Walk-Away Position in action, consider a common fact pattern involving settlement negotiations stemming from a personal injury suit. Assume the plaintiff suffered extensive injuries when her car was hit broadside by a speeding truck operated by the employee of a small, privately held corporation. The accident occurred about thirty minutes after sundown during a driving rainstorm. There is an eyewitness willing to testify that the truck driver ran a stop sign. The driver claims the sign was difficult to see due to darkness and poor weather conditions. He also claims that the plaintiff was not using her headlights, thus making the plaintiff's car difficult to see. The plaintiff's medical expenses total $4500. The plaintiff has filed suit against the driver and his employer seeking to recover $125,000 in general and special damages. The defendant has responded with a general denial and an affirmative defense based on comparative negligence. The plaintiff's attorney has determined that the company's liability insurance policy has a limit of $100,000. The plaintiff is eager for a quick cash settlement. The insurance company has disputed the plaintiff's special damages. Based on the foregoing information, the plaintiff and her attorney must formulate a realistic Walk-Away Position in terms of the minimum amount they would be willing to accept in settlement of the claim. The alternative to a settlement is a lengthy trial and possible appeal.

The facts indicate that the plaintiff enjoys a relatively strong position regarding the issue of the defendant's liability. The primary weakness relates to the defense of comparative negligence. The plaintiff's attorney knows that for practical purposes the policy limit of $100,000 establishes an absolute ceiling on any settlement with the defendant's insurance carrier. He also knows that any actual settlement will probably be substantially lower than the policy limits. This particular insurance company does not have the reputation of an easy settler, but in clear-cut cases of liability will, after some bargaining, offer between three to five times special damages. The attorney also knows that discovery and trial would take about a year and that an appeal could consume another twelve to fifteen months. Finally, he knows there is never any certainty of what a jury might do, especially in light of his client's alleged failure to use her headlights.

In light of all this information, the plaintiff estimates that the case has a minimum settlement value of $13,500 with a maximum of $30,000. After allowing for a reduction of $2500 to encourage a quick settlement and provide a buffer against miscalculation, the plaintiff's counsel arrives at an initial Walk-Away Position of $11,000. He also knows that this figure is subject to fluctuation during the discovery phase and ensuing settlement negotiations. At any point in the bargaining, if the plaintiff's attorney is convinced that the insurance company's final offer will fall below $11,000 or a sum representing the then-current bottom-line position, the plaintiff would be prepared to activate the Walk-Away Position and take her chances at trial. Of course, all of this assumes that the client is willing to accept her attorney's advice. Assuming she is, the Walk-Away Position is poised in readiness.

In this example, the Walk-Away Position was determined by such factors as the strength and value of the claim, the settlement patterns of the insurance company, the verdict expectancy in the particular jurisdiction and the willingness to accept the calculated risk of trial and appeal. Unfortunately, even this seemingly sophisticated assessment is an educated guess.

Practice tip: As uncertain as the procedure of calculating a Walk-Away Position is, it's always preferable to the alternative of having no alternative.

CAPITALIZING ON THE DEFENSIVE LEVERAGE ADVANTAGES OF THE WALK-AWAY POSITION

Once you have analyzed the situation, identified your alternatives, and formulated your Walk-Away Position, you have created a potentially powerful defensive leverage advantage. By accepting the possibility that the negotiation could fail to achieve your objectives and identifying your alternatives at the outset, you deprive your opponent of much of the effective use of the leverage of uncertainty. You have psychologically insulated yourself from failure. You have also allowed yourself the luxury of making difficult decisions objectively without being subjected to the pressures of a crisis situation. Consequently, if and when a crisis comes, you will have already developed a well-reasoned alternative course of action. This tends to deprive the opponent of leverage involving sanctions, uncertainty and the use of deadlines.

THE WALK-AWAY POSITION AS LEVERAGE IN RESERVE

In addition to the defensive aspects of the Walk-Away Position, it is also a powerful offensive leverage device. A credible threat to break off talks and seek alternative courses of action can create a high degree of uncertainty in the mind of your opponent. As a result, communicating your Walk-Away Position can often turn the tables on an opponent and extract concessions neither party thought possible. This equalizing effect has the potential to change the entire character and momentum of a negotiation. This is simply one more reason why developing a Walk-Away Position should receive high priority in all of your prenegotiation organization and planning.

OBJECTIVITY, REALISM, AND FLEXIBILITY ARE MUSTS

Developing a workable Walk-Away Position requires an objective and realistic analysis of the circumstances confronting you. Because miscalculation is an ever-present danger, you should strive to avoid the dangers of subjectivity, unfounded optimism, and acting on insufficient information. As previously suggested, it is also vitally important to remain flexible and be willing to adjust your Walk-Away Position as the negotiation unfolds. It is often helpful to view your Walk-Away Position as you would a share of common stock. The price of the stock fluctuates depending on any number of tangible and intangible factors. The same is true of the Walk-Away Position. In our personal injury example, failure to locate a key witness, discovery of low insurance limits, or a sudden need for cash by your client can cause you to lower your Walk-Away Position. By the same token, uncovering damaging evidence against the defendant, an ill-advised admission, or an internal deadline working against your opponent can drive up the Walk-Away Position. In either event, failure to adjust your position accordingly can lead to a disastrous result.

DON'T MAKE THREATS YOU CAN'T BACK UP

Communicating your Walk-Away Position is a utilization of leverage. Actually activating it is abandonment of the entire bargaining relationship. This is why you must carefully weigh all of the implications of communicating or activating the Walk-Away Position. The quickest way to lose your credibility is to make a threat you aren't willing or able to back up. This is why you should take extreme care to not only calculate your Walk-Away Position, but also to communicate it in an informational tone rather than as a threat or ultimatum.

Practice tip: If and when you do decide to walk away from a negotiation, make sure you are willing and able to move to a workable alternative. Nothing is worse than walking out on a negotiation only to return a day or a week later with hat in hand. You rarely get a second chance under such circumstances.

MASTERING THE PRINCIPLES OF CONTINGENCY PLANNING

While the Walk-Away Position can be an invaluable offensive and defensive negotiating weapon, it is certainly not the only Fallback Technique available to you. Short-run or tactical fallback techniques based on the principles of contingency planning should play an integral role in the preparation and execution of any negotiation plan.

ANTICIPATION AND FLEXIBILITY: THE KEYS TO CONTINGENCY PLANNING

Unfortunately, too many overly optimistic negotiators overlook the reality that things don't ever go their way 100 percent of the time. Consequently, they fail to formulate contingency plans to deal with setbacks that are almost sure to occur. When problems do occur, the negotiator is unprepared to deal with them effectively. Decisions aimed at coping with reversals and setbacks are often made under extreme pressure. Because of the crisis atmosphere, available options and alternative courses of action are often ill-defined or overlooked. The consequence is a reactive approach to tactical decision making. The results are often predictable and many times disastrous.

Anticipation and flexibility are the two keys to combatting problems inherent in crisis decision making. By anticipating the tactical moves and responses your opponent is likely to make, you are in a position to act affirmatively by devising well-thought-out Fallback measures of your own. By building flexibility into your negotiating plan, you are able to create effective short-term safety valves and escape hatches to deal with reversals in much the same way that the Walk-Away Position provides a strategic safety net under your long-term negotiating objectives.

HOW TO BUILD IN A TIME CUSHION

When planning a timeframe for concluding an agreement, operate under the premise that "everything takes more time than you think." You only need to look through dates of correspondence relating to past negotiations in some of your old files to confirm the wisdom of this statement. The best way to cope with this eventuality is to build in a time cushion whenever possible. You can do this in a number of ways.

THE DOUBLE DEADLINE: YOURS AND THEIRS

A favorite approach is to set your own deadline for agreement while announcing an earlier one to your opponent. Conversely, always try to anticipate the opposition's external and internal deadline.

AVOIDING THE LAST-MINUTE CRUNCH

A second approach to building in a time cushion is to be conscious of the leverage of timing regarding the pressure of deadlines and to respond by trying to accelerate the pace of a negotiation so as to avoid or minimize the leverage of timing that could be exerted against you and your client.

PLAN AHEAD FOR ALTERNATIVE COURSES OF ACTION

A third technique for building in extra time is to identify alternatives and consider different courses of action, and anticipate actions and possible reasons of your opponents in advance. This tends to insulate you from the dangers of formulating positions and selecting alternatives under unfavorable conditions. This approach makes maximum productive use of your time and avoids the tendency to make concessions in crisis situations.

DEVELOP SHORT-TERM FALLBACK POSITIONS

In addition to the foregoing measures, you should constantly be developing short-term Fallback Positions as the negotiation unfolds.

This requires application of the same principles that govern formulation of the Walk-Away Position. The only difference is that Short-Term Fallback Planning involves anticipation of an opponent's moves at each stage of the bargaining with a corresponding alternative response.

ASKING AND GETTING

For instance, assume you are attempting to sell a parcel of land. After many offers and counteroffers, you and the attorney for the potential buyer are still $2000 apart. At this point, you decide to make a final offer. Because you are so close in price, you know you will not invoke your Walk-Away Position. Nevertheless, you would like to close the price differential as much as possible. Based on the negotiations, you know that if you offered to reduce the price by $1500, the buyer would almost surely increase his offer by $500. Consequently, this should represent your ultimate Short-Term Fallback. Confident that you could conclude the agreement on this basis, you decide to reduce your price by $500 on the chance that the prospective buyer might accept it or, alternatively, make a counterproposal to split the difference by upping his offer by $1000 if you would drop the asking price by $1000. Should both of these approaches fail, you know what your ultimate Fallback would be to ensure a deal without an undue delay of time.

Practice tip: This very basic principle is just one more application of contingency planning. Those negotiators who take the extra time to plan for inevitable long- and short-term setbacks will find themselves in a position of control even when things are not going exactly according to plan. Anticipating problems and formulating contingent responses is the best way to head off a crisis and insulate yourself from the pressures that will result when you are confronted by a setback.

WHAT TO DO WHEN YOU'RE ON THE ROPES

All the contingency planning and positive thinking in the world can't help you in those situations in which you are outgunned at every turn. Every lawyer has experienced that feeling of helplessness when confronted by an opponent armed with superior leverage, favorable law and facts, numerous alternatives to a negotiated agreement, and all the time in the world in which to make a decision. When faced with such overwhelming circumstances, there is little you can do to turn the tables on a vastly superior opponent. On the other hand, just because you're on the ropes doesn't mean the situation is hopeless. There are techniques and principles that negotiators can use to make the best out of a bad situation. This section is devoted to dealing with those unpleasant and hopefully infrequent situations in which the question is not whether you will win or lose, but rather how bad is it going to be.

DON'T MAKE A BAD SITUATION WORSE

Often you are in a dilemma due to circumstances over which you have no control. In others, your predicament might be due to poor planning, a tactical mistake, acting on insufficient information, or any number of other reasons related to the conduct of the negotiation. Regardless of the cause of your problem, you want to ensure that you don't add fuel to the fire or compound your troubles. One sure way to do exactly what you don't want to do is to fall victim to the pressure generated by earlier reversals. While we acknowledge that the advice "Don't panic" is easy to give and tougher to follow, there are antipanic techniques that can be used in even the most nightmarish situations.

BUY TIME TO IDENTIFY ALTERNATIVES
AND SLOW YOUR OPPONENT'S MOMENTUM

One of the best ways to avoid getting into deeper trouble is to buy time to identify alternatives and analyze the consequences of your actions as well as those of your opponent. Additionally, buying time can often help slow or even halt the momentum of the other side. In some cases, circumstances may change with time. In others, you may be only staving off the inevitable, but at least you will be able to prepare for it or possibly work out more advantageous concession terms. In any event, you rarely stand to lose by employing delay tactics in this type of losing situation.

HE'S OUT OF THE OFFICE

There are numerous time-buying techniques. The most effective is simply to not be available when the other side wants to negotiate. Business trips, outside appointments, attendance at meetings are all sure-fire ways of avoiding confrontation with the other side. Call it stalling, delay, unavailability, or whatever else you choose, it works.

THE CHECK IS IN THE MAIL

Whether the other side is looking for a check, an offer, a response, or an answer, the mail is a wonderful way to buy time. Correspondence takes time. If you want to delay, use the mail.

THE JAMMED SCHEDULE

A third time-buying technique is the Jammed Schedule. "I'd love to sit down with you to resolve your client's problem. Let's see, I'm out of town next week, I will be in court the week after, I have to take some depositions after that...I'll get back to you when my schedule opens up."

DISCOVERY AND PROCEDURE

If you are involved in litigation, discovery is a potent and effective way to supplement the negotiating process. It provides a vehicle for uncovering new or additional facts that can swing the momentum in your favor. By its very nature, the process is also time-consuming. This can prove to be a benefit to a negotiator who is in no hurry to go to trial.

COMBINING DELAY TACTICS

Lawyers representing debtors, defendants, and other target parties have raised delay to an art form. Back-to-back business trips sandwiched in between meetings, depositions, and court appearances woven around a lengthy exchange of correspondence is an excellent way to buy an extra month or two.

DON'T PLAY TO STRENGTHS

When you finally are forced to negotiate under adverse circumstances, you should make every effort to avoid your opponent's strengths. If you are representing a defendant in a personal injury suit involving clear-cut liability and uncertain damages, talk about damages. Point out to the opposing attorney that proving liability will do his client little good if there are no damages.

If you are weak as to supporting legal precedent, argue the facts. If your opponent enjoys superiority as to the facts and the substantive law, divert the discussion to points of procedure. This is just another way to offset the other party's momentum and delay the final outcome. On occasion, you can divert the direction of the entire negotiation to the point that the original focus is either lost altogether or the opponent's position and leverage are made to appear less persuasive or powerful than they really are.

INVOKE UNCERTAINTY

Even when you're on the ropes, the aggressor is subject to the leverage of uncertainty. Planting a seed of doubt, even if there is little basis for it, can help stem the tide of a negotiation. Leading the other side to believe your position is stronger than it actually is can help stave off defeat.

Practice tip: This is one of the few situations in which you might want to risk a bluff that you know you can't back up. If defeat is inevitable, there is probably little to lose and a great deal to gain.

PLAY THE WALK-AWAY CARD

As discussed previously, the ultimate Fallback when you're on the ropes is to play your Walk-Away Card. Unfortunately, this is not always a viable alternative. However, when faced with the choice of reaching an agreement with the devil or walking away into the deep blue sea, a swim may be in order.

CONCESSION BEHAVIOR: THE BEST WAY TO LOSE

No lawyer is invincible. For whatever the reason, every attorney has occasionally found himself on the short end of a negotiation. However, even when defeat is inevitable there is always something that can be done to improve your position. There is a best way to lose based on concession behavior principles and techniques that you can employ immediately. Hopefully, you won't have to resort to these tactics anytime soon, but when a bad day at the bargaining table rolls around, and it will, you will be ready to salvage something for yourself and your client. While it's not your first or even second choice, a qualified surrender beats an unconditional surrender every time.

GET SOMETHING IN RETURN FOR YOUR CONCESSION

Always remember that a negotiation is never over until the ink is dry on the agreement. This means that if you must yield to your opponent's demands, try to extract something in return. For example, if you represent a client who owes $20,000 on a secured note and you are forced to pay back the full amount in order to avoid foreclosure, there are still options available to you. One approach is to admit liability and offer to "work with the bank to ensure full satisfaction of the debt." This might take the form of negotiating installment payments, receiving a limited extension so that funds may be raised, or renewing the loan if additional collateral can be given. Surprisingly, once you concede liability, the lender will make concessions of its own. The reason is simple. The bank doesn't want the collateral if it can get its money. By conceding liability and assuming the role of mediator, the bank has new-found hope that it will eventually get its money, which is all it wanted in the first place.

CAN YOU HELP ME OUT?

Another application of getting something of value for your concession is illustrated by the termination of a commercial contract. If all else fails and you are unable to talk the other side out of exercising its right to terminate, you may want to take the following approach: "Well, Bill, I'm really sorry your client feels that he has to terminate. Losing this order will really hurt my client. Tell you what, it sure would cushion the blow if you could help us avoid the adverse publicity by keeping this out of the trade magazines." This request will cost the disgruntled customer little or nothing, but could be of real benefit to the client in terms of preserving the confidence of other customers. Assuming such a request is handled properly, the chances are good that the victor will accommodate the losing party.

CONTAIN YOUR LOSSES

The preceding example also underscores another crucial point. If you have to lose, contain your losses as much as possible. In the foregoing example, one customer has been lost; however, the quick-thinking attorney took steps to cut the client's loss of customers at once. While the lost business hurts, the potential adverse publicity could have been disastrous.

DON'T THROW IN THE TOWEL— ONLY PIECES OF IT

When things really look bleak, there is a tendency to become frustrated and overreact. Consequently, when some negotiators see the handwriting on the wall, they react by throwing in the towel. Sometimes such total surrender is justified, sometimes it's not. The best approach is to concede one point at a time, starting with the least important and moving to the most important. As a result, the other party may cease their demands short of taking everything for a variety of reasons. Sympathy is one. A perception that the well is dry when it's not is another.

CONCEDING A DEAL POINT TO SAVE ANOTHER

A variation of sequential concessions involves the concept of making a partial concession look like a total victory for the opposition. This involves conceding an obvious Deal Point in exchange for an agreement. The agreement appears to be a total victory for the other side; however, in fact, the final agreement provides for the attainment of some less obvious, albeit important objectives for your client.

INFLATE THE WORTH OF THE CONCESSION

If you must concede an important point to get an agreement, the circumstances might call for you to inflate the value of the concession to the other party as a way of foregoing continued bargaining that could reveal other weaknesses in your position. This technique is also helpful in extracting something of value in return for your concession.

MASK THE DAMAGE

Conversely, the circumstances may require that you mask the damage caused by your concessions or minimize the importance it has on your client. This is true in situations where the true extent of the damage done could reveal other weaknesses in your position or undermine long-term objectives of your client. Examples include revelations that could erode public confidence in your client, disclosure of cash-flow problems, or other internal problems.

KEEP YOUR CLIENT INFORMED

From the client's standpoint, the best way to emerge smelling like a rose from a losing situation is to keep him informed every step of the way. Surveys indicate that client satisfaction has little to do with the results their lawyers are able to accomplish for them. Rather, it is the attitude of the attorney toward his client and problem, and the willingness to keep the client appraised of the situation, that counted most. This is why you should consult your client every step of the way. Document the progress or lack of it in a negotiation with phone calls, letters, and meetings. Always present your client with a realistic picture of what is happening and what is likely to happen, as well as his available alternatives. Finally, be honest about where he stands and what his chances are. If the situation looks bad, prepare your client for the worst. Conversely, if the situation initially looks good, still prepare him for the worst. Things change, and when they do, no surprise is a good surprise.

KEEP IT PROFESSIONAL

Finally, you should always face defeat as professionally as you accept victory. Yelling, swearing, or crying won't do you a lot of good at this point. Remember, there will be other battles, often with the same players. When that happens, you will be remembered not so much for winning or losing, but for how you handled it. Just because you lost a round doesn't mean you have to forfeit your reputation. Keeping things on a professional basis will ensure that you don't.

11

Closing

The outcome of months of investigation, meetings, phone calls, letters, and document drafts can hinge on what is done or said over the span of only a few minutes. At this point, the only thing that counts is the ability to get the other side to say the magic word, yes. All that has gone on before adds up to zero if the parties are unable to pin down a final, binding agreement. Every lawyer has at least one sad story about the big one that got away. In many of these situations, the deal was lost because of an inability to close.

Because closing is so dependent on one's sense of judgment and timing, and because every negotiation differs in terms of issues, parties and leverage, it is very difficult to lay down hard and fast rules. However, we can point out the factors present in every closing and suggest some basic approaches and techniques aimed at making you more effective in the clutch.

WHEN IS THE RIGHT TIME
TO CLOSE A NEGOTIATION?

The right time to close a negotiation is when everyone is ready, willing, and able to say yes to all of the terms embodied in a proposed agreement. Conversely, the wrong time is any other time. The problem lies in pinpointing the right time to close. Your sense of timing and judgment become critical in making this determination.

DEADLINES CAN DICTATE
THE RIGHT TIME FOR CLOSING

In certain negotiations, internal or external deadlines will dictate the right time to close negotiation. For instance, in a collective bargain-

173

ing negotiation in which the alternative to an agreement is a strike, the external deadline for closing is almost always the expiration of the contract term then in existence. In other situations, such as where one of the parties is seeking to take advantage of certain tax considerations, the internal deadline for agreement would be just prior to the end of his fiscal year for tax purposes.

In those situations where a deadline for an agreement is a factor, identifying the appropriate time for closing is a relatively simple matter. Once the deadline is identified, the rest will become fairly obvious. For instance, in our example of the party operating under an internal deadline to take advantage of certain tax deductions, the correct approach would be to use delay tactics to extend the time for closing rather than agree to an earlier closing date the other party will doubtlessly be seeking. In this case, your final offer should coincide with the other party's internal deadline. When the opposition is faced with the choice of making certain concessions to guarantee an agreement versus the risk of reaching no agreement and thus losing all tax benefits, they will most likely make the concessions to close the deal.

HOW TO PUSH THE TRANSACTION TO A CONCLUSION

The more difficult situation involves negotiations in which there is little or no deadline pressure to close. In this type of case, it will be up to one or both of the parties to determine the appropriate time to conclude the agreement. Usually, the party with the superior leverage will be in the most advantageous position to specify the time for closing. However, awareness of the time for closing can be used to offset this advantage.

To illustrate, assume a buyer and seller are negotiating the purchase and sale of a certain parcel of commercial real estate. The particular parcel is not a prime piece of land in terms of location. The prospective purchaser is considering several sites. The seller has no other prospective buyers. The original asking price is $200,000 with a 20 percent down payment, which is competitive with the terms being asked by the owners of the other comparable parcels of land. The parties are in basic agreement as to all terms except price and financing. The buyer wants to pay less than $200,000, with the cheapest possible financing. While neither party is in any particular hurry, the seller knows that continued dickering will serve no purpose other than to provide the prospective buyer more time in which to find a significantly better alternative in terms of price and interest rate. The buyer and seller both have reason to believe that mortgage interest rates will probably drop gradually in the coming months.

Based on these facts, the seller knows that the buyer has little to gain by closing a deal now. He also knows that his chances to make a deal will diminish with time. As a result, the seller decides to take a calculated risk to push for a deal. He decides to tell the prospective buyer that for personal reasons he has to make a deal by the end of the week or be forced to withdraw the property from the market. Knowing this will probably not be enough to ensure a deal, he offers to reduce the price by $5000 and the down payment by 5 percent and agree that the first payment will be due in six months so as to allow the buyer to finance the deal at a possible lower rate of interest.

This action on the part of the seller now requires either a response or a counteroffer from the buyer. In lieu of a positive response, the seller must be prepared to take the property off the market and lose a potential sale, at least for the time being.

THE BUYER'S POSSIBLE RESPONSES

Let's analyze the possible responses by the buyer: *Yes*—Here, the seller has assured a deal by giving up $5000 on the purchase price, $10,000 in front money, and six months of time before the first payment is due. This illustrates the old adage that 95 percent of something beats 100 percent of nothing every time.

COUNTEROFFER BY BUYER

Here the seller has the option to close on new terms proposed by the buyer, or answer the counteroffer with a counterproposal of his own in the context of the one-week deadline set earlier by the seller. *No*—The seller would remove the property from the market, at least for the time being. Here the seller has lost little. He can always put the property back on the market within a reasonable period of time. The only thing the seller wants to guard against is a loss of credibility in the eyes of the buyer. When the property does go back on the market, the seller may ultimately reach agreement with this or another buyer. In the meantime, the seller has lost very little since there were no other prospective buyers in the first place.

THE THREE DON'TS OF CLOSING

In situations such as the previous example, in which there is little or no deadline pressure, it will be incumbent on you to take the initiative to guide the transaction to a close. The only words of warning in this regard can be summarized in terms of the three don'ts of closing:

1. *Don't* press for a closing until you have all the relevant information to make an intelligent offer or an informed response to an offer.

2. *Don't* press for a closing if you feel the other side is not ready to close and would view your efforts with mistrust or suspicion. Being premature or overanxious can scare the other side away from a deal they would otherwise be willing to make.

3. *Don't* allow the other side to press for a closing until you are ready to close. Too many people find themselves swept into deals they were not ready to make by falling victim to closing tactics used against them.

FOUR PROVEN CLOSING TECHNIQUES

Once you are ready to close but feel the other side is in no hurry, there are several techniques available to help guide the negotiation to a conclusion.

SUMMARIZATION

This is a time-tested technique in which the party ready to close simply repeats all the elements of the deal in summary form, concluding with phrases such as:

"This is my understanding of the terms. If you are in agreement, I can have the documents prepared." Or:

"Unless you have anything to add, that should wrap it up.... Do we have a deal?" Or:

Something else to that effect together with the customary extended hand to seal the agreement with the symbolic handshake.

MARATHON

The "Marathon" approach is often used when the parties still have a number of differences. A final meeting is scheduled After numerous cups of coffee have been consumed and ashtrays have long since been filled, the party seeking to close will finally say something like "Look, we've been here for hours and at this rate we could be here days from now. We agree on most of the important matters. Let's split the difference on the remaining issues and go home."

Practice tip: This technique has a better chance of succeeding depending on the lateness of the hour and how close the parties actually are on the major issues.

ALL OR NOTHING

This technique involves a calculated risk to break an impasse and reach an agreement. When there appears to be genuine deadlock, the party seeking to close offers his last trade point or another concession that he has been holding in reserve. He couples this offer with an announcement that "This is the very best I can do. As far as I'm concerned, it comes down to this or nothing. Either you meet me halfway or let's just forget everything."

Practice tip: Of course, there is a risk that the other party will respond to the "All or Nothing" ultimatum with a "That's just fine with me. Let's forget it." This is why the All or Nothing ploy should be a technique of last resort.

THE MULTIPLE CHOICE PLOY

Once we were negotiating a settlement agreement on behalf of an entertainer who sued a resort hotel claiming anticipatory repudiation of a performance contract. It was obvious that the hotel would be held liable if the case went to trial. It was also clear that neither the plaintiff nor defendant wanted a trial. The defense lawyer was dragging his feet in making a final decision settling the case. We surmised that since the hotel was in a beach resort area, it was probably waiting until the summer months when it would have a better cash flow and could more easily absorb a settlement. It was also obvious that the hotel wanted to forego any payment for as long as possible. In order to break the impasse and conclude the agreement, we used the "Multiple Choice" Ploy. Our offer was couched in the following alternatives:

1. The plaintiff will accept $15,000 now, or
2. $16,000 within thirty days, or
3. $17,000 within sixty days, or
4. $20,000 spread over six months.

The combination of offering the defendant a delayed payment plan, combined with the power of suggestion, worked. "Here are the four alternatives. It's up to you to choose one." After thinking it over, the hotel chose alternative 3. The case was settled.

ONCE THE OTHER SIDE SAYS YES... STOP!

Besides never getting around to concluding the deal, the biggest mistake negotiators make in closing is not knowing when to quit. Once the other party has agreed to your terms, *stop!* Too many people continue to sell the deal after it's been sold. This tends to have the effect of scaring the other side away, of disclosing additional information that makes the other side rethink their position or of reopening topics already agreed upon for further negotiation.

The best way to guard against overclosing is to shake hands, promise to have the paperwork delivered for signature as soon as possible, and leave. If the transaction is over the telephone, simply conclude the conversation. This makes it impossible to talk yourself out of what you spent so much time talking yourself into.

DON'T PROCRASTINATE ON THE PAPERWORK

Because most agreements involve a written contract, or a court or consent order before the transaction is finalized, it's important not to drag your feet on the paperwork. By the same token, don't let the other side cause problems by their own delay. The best way to take care of this is to (1) volunteer to do the drafting, and (2) make the drafting your top priority.

Practice tip: If the other side insists upon doing the drafting, don't hesitate to prod them. Create a sense of urgency or use a deadline such as a business trip or court appearance to spur the other side to take action.

THE SECONDARY NEGOTIATION

Even though you have reached the handshake stage, the transaction is never concluded until the papers are signed. More than one handshake deal has fallen apart due to bickering over the details of the final document. Naturally, some of this is unavoidable; however, there are measures you can take to minimize the chances of this happening.

HOW TO ENSURE SUCCESS IN THE SECONDARY NEGOTIATION

Once the deal is concluded, repeat the major elements of the transaction at the closing to make sure there have been no misunderstandings. If there have been, straighten them out on the spot rather than giving the other side time to mull them over and reflect on areas in which there might be a difference of opinion or interpretation.

If the deal requires detailed drafting, follow the oral agreement with a letter of understanding or agreement in principle summarizing all major points in writing. Whenever possible, have all parties sign the letter pending formal execution of the more detailed documents.

When drafting, be absolutely true to the letter and spirit of what the parties have agreed to. There is nothing more potentially damaging than trying to slip a major point into the agreement that is inconsistent with what the parties have approved. The entire basis of trust between the parties will be destroyed if the other side suspects that you are trying to put one over on him.

When dealing with points germane to the agreement but which have not been expressly addressed such as audit rights, indemnity, etc., you should draft language to benefit your client whenever possible while at the same time being fair and not providing points that can become major issues of dispute. It's always best to negotiate these points with opposing counsel before the terms are submitted to the clients. This technique allows points of disagreement in the secondary negotiation to be contained between the lawyers. It also ensures that the lawyers will present a united front to their clients on these relatively minor matters, thus guarding against a last-minute snag that could kill the deal.

Practice tip: In all your drafting and secondary negotiations, you should be guided by good judgment, discretion, and fair dealing. Also remember that most of the time the other lawyer doesn't want last-minute problems any more than you do. This is why you should contain your differences whenever possible and not give opposing counsel reason to have to reopen the negotiation at the client level.

BE A GOOD WINNER
AND DOWNPLAY YOUR SUCCESS

Regardless of whether the negotiation involves a long-term business agreement or the settlement of bitter litigation, if you have gotten the better of things be a good winner. You should do or say whatever is necessary to leave the other side in a good frame of mind without becoming patronizing. A sincere word of commendation for the other lawyer for how he handled the negotiation, or a letter putting in a good word for the opposing client, never hurts. Rubbing the opposition's nose in what may be a less than satisfactory agreement is a guaranteed way to make enemies for yourself and your client and create trouble down the line. If you must gloat about your successes, don't do it at the expense of the opposition—it will surely come back to haunt you.

DON'T OVERREACH

This point is of special importance in business transactions. As we will discuss in Chapter Twelve on "Deal Making," imposing an unduly onerous contract on the other side even when you have the leverage to do it is a hollow victory that can sow the seeds for trouble later on. It's in the best long-term interest of both you and your client to negotiate deals that work in practice and not just on paper.

Overreaching is less of a concern in litigation settlements because there are fewer long-term implications. However, from the standpoint of your own future you should be gracious in victory. You will certainly appreciate the same type of treatment when you're handed the short end of the stick.

BE A GOOD LOSER
WHEN YOU HAVE TO LOSE

When the short end of the stick does present itself, and it will, be professional about it. Tantrums and derogatory remarks won't reverse the damage, but they can help contribute to future problems.

THERE IS ALWAYS A RIGHT WAY TO WIN AND LOSE

Always remember that your integrity and credibility as an attorney is one of your most important assets. Reputations are never built overnight but can be destroyed in a single day. No matter how the bottom line is tallied in a single negotiation, you can rest assured that you will have numerous opportunities in the future to put your negotiation skills and talents to work. Your credibility and reputation will play an important part in your future success. The element of your character can be enhanced only by learning the right way to win and lose

12

Deal Making: Guidelines for Successful Business Negotiation

Spearheading mergers, brokering acquisitions, and dickering over every kind of license, assignment, and contract clause imaginable falls to the specialist known as the business lawyer. Whether working in a corporate legal department or with a private firm, the lawyer with an office practice frequently must rely more on his ability to shape consensus and manage compromise than on traditional legal training and knowledge. A close look at the time sheets of some of the most successful business practitioners reveals many spend the bulk of their time negotiating rather than practicing law. One well-known attorney who specializes in the representation of professional athletes summed up the relationship between law and negotiation in a business setting as follows: "We all know the terms, clauses, and percentages by heart; it's simply a matter of how much you can get the other side to give up short of blowing the deal."

THE TWO MEASURES OF SUCCESS IN A BUSINESS NEGOTIATION

Lawyers negotiating on behalf of business clients are measured by two important criteria: (1) the ability to strike a deal, and (2) the quality of that deal. Success or failure in either regard is computed in dollars and cents. Businesspeople accountable to corporate superiors, directors, and stockholders can ill afford to tolerate lawyers who are unable to succeed consistently at striking profitable deals for their clients. This is precisely why the stock in trade of a successful business lawyer is his ability to negotiate.

BUSINESS BARGAINING IS DIFFERENT

Negotiating contracts, licenses, and acquisitions differs significantly from settling lawsuits or labor disputes in terms of approach, objectives, negotiating style, and application of leverage. Sharpening one's skills in the business arena requires an understanding and appreciation of these differences. For this reason, it is appropriate to focus on the important recurring patterns and characteristics common to most, if not all, business negotiations.

EVERYONE HAS SOMETHING TO GAIN

Business negotiators approach a negotiation with much greater optimism than do lawyers engaged in lawsuit, strike settlement, or other conflict resolution negotiations. This is because everyone usually has something to gain from a potential business deal. Otherwise, they would not be wasting their time negotiating. In business situations, the alternative to agreement is rarely a jury trial or strike, but rather a lost opportunity. This is not to say the ramifications of failing to reach an agreement are not sometimes serious and in certain instances potentially catastrophic. However, such is usually not the case. Consequently, the overall tone of most business negotiations is usually upbeat.

The type and degree of potential gain will vary with the needs and circumstances of the parties. It may involve realization of such tangible advantages as increasing cash flow, diversifying production, acquiring know-how and expertise, purchasing a distribution network or the right to use a trademark. Less tangible and more indirect objectives may include attainment of prestige, improved community relations or higher corporate visibility. Regardless of the type of gain sought, the upbeat tone and prospect of mutual gain in the business area makes Give-to-Get negotiating preferable to other approaches. This is in marked contrast to litigation in which the plaintiff's success is usually attained at the expense of the defendant. In litigation, the defendant is a winner only if he can prevent the plaintiff from succeeding. Even if the defendant scores a complete victory, he has only preserved the status quo. It's not difficult to understand defendant's overwhelming lack of enthusiasm for win-win negotiation when his position is viewed in this context.

WHY WIN-WIN WORKS IN BUSINESS

Because everyone stands to gain in business bargaining, there is a much greater likelihood that the parties will be more committed to a negotiated solution. On the other hand, each stands to lose in terms of time and opportunity if no agreement results. The prospect of mutual rather than unilateral gain makes problem solving and compromise much more attractive. As a result, ultimatums and harsh words are much more likely to send an opponent out the door rather than to his knees.

Practice tip: Hardball negotiating style stressing an "I win, you lose" approach is much less likely to succeed in the realm of business than it might in litigation settlement talks.

WHY YOU SHOULD STRIVE TO ENHANCE PERSONAL RELATIONSHIPS IN A BUSINESS NEGOTIATION

Because so many business contracts require ongoing reciprocal performance, continuing good faith between the parties is essential. This is certainly true in employment, distribution, sales, or supply contracts. Even in corporate takeovers or acquisitions, good will is necessary to accomplish a smooth transition and to ensure that trade secrets and other valuable information are effectively and accurately disclosed. This is why preserving personal relationships is almost always an important underlying consideration for the business negotiator.

DON'T BE AFRAID TO GET TOUGH WHEN THE CIRCUMSTANCES DICTATE

The roles mutuality and good faith play in the long-term success of business agreements underscore the need to approach this type of negotiation in a cooperative manner which stresses personal rapport, common solutions, and equitable compromise whenever possible. This is not to imply that Hardball tactics and the leverage of sanction should never be utilized. Adopting a hard line when toughness is called for may be the only way to preserve your client's integrity and ensure against unnecessary concessions. There is a dangerous tendency to confuse fairness with appeasement and rapport with avoiding tough issues. As stated earlier, the controlling principle governing your negotiating approach, strategy, and tactics should be flexibility and what's best for the client over the long as well as near term. This means reading the circumstances and taking action calculated to serve those interests most effectively.

Practice tip: Based on the recurrent characteristics of most business negotiations, you likely will find yourself being more successful by stressing the positive and avoiding the negative. However, you should be prepared to get tough when the circumstances dictate.

HOW TO PLAN FOR
A BUSINESS NEGOTIATION

Planning for a business negotiation can be decidedly more difficult and time-consuming than in other types of negotiations. The number and type of bargaining issues tend to be more wide ranging, encompassing a much greater spectrum of possible objectives and facts. All of these must be identified, factored, and injected into the substantive talks. Candid and thorough conferences with your client will help identify his objectives, limitations, and time constraints. From this you should be able to set up preliminary Deal Points, Secondary Points, and Trade Points. This should also allow you to make an initial assessment of actual and potential leverage and provide basis for constructing strategic approach for the Opening Move supported by tactical maneuvers. Finally, you should force your client to develop a Walk-Away Position should the negotiations fail.

SELLING FALLBACK STRATEGY TO YOUR CLIENT

Forcing the client to develop a Walk-Away Position can be a real sticking point with optimistic businesspeople who are convinced that "nothing can go wrong." This type of client is often more interested in counting his money rather than planning for trouble. Making the client deal with problem areas and potential failure is often viewed by the client as "negativism" or "lack of aggressiveness" on the part of the lawyer. Experienced attorneys know better, although it's often a challenge to explain this to the client. While there is no proven way to bring a "Get-Rich-Quick" client back down to earth, there are some time-tested approaches that can help you get the point across.

"I'm paid to worry": The success of this approach rests on how effective you are at pointing out to your client that he is paying a lot of money to let you do his worrying for him. You should stress your

genuine concern for the client and his affairs. This approach should be concluded with the standard disclaimer that is generally effective in getting him to go along: "Well, if the deal turns out to be as profitable as you feel it will, we can all laugh about this meeting when I run into you at the bank. On the other hand, worrying now won't cost you anything extra, but it could save you a lot later."

The horror story: An alternate and somewhat more dramatic approach is the horror story. You simply relate two or three unfortunate stories of clients involved in "Can't Miss" deals who refused to develop contingency plans to guard against stalled negotiations. The rest should take care of itself. It always helps your credibility if one or more of these former business whiz kids is operating an elevator or parking cars in close proximity to your office. Depending on how good a storyteller you are, this approach will usually get the job done.

Sizing up the opposition: This is usually the toughest part of planning for a business negotiation. The primary reason for this is the range and complexity of personalities, objectives, issues, and decision makers involved in the business negotiation. To illustrate, assume that X Corporation, a major high technology firm, has expressed an interest in acquiring your client, a small research and development firm specializing in solar technology, complete with patents, trade secrets, and employment agreements with key personnel. Further assume that your client would be interested in the deal provided X Corporation is willing to pay top dollar and further provided there weren't other factors that would mitigate against selling. Insight into the personalities, motives, and circumstances behind X Corporation's offer will strongly influence the ultimate decision as to whether to enter into negotiations to sell and, if so, under what terms.

WHY DOES THE OTHER SIDE WANT THE DEAL?

This is one of the first questions you should ask yourself. In our example, the reasons are potentially wide ranging and significant. One possible explanation could be that X Corporation is engaged in an ongoing expansion program through acquisitions; or (2) X Corporation might be looking for an end of the year acquisition to reduce its tax liability; or (3) they might be seeking to buy knowhow in the form of trade secrets or patents which could just as easily be licensed; or (4) they could be seeking to purchase a specific invention or patent application that could provide them with the necessary link to make a major breakthrough which would result in significant profits.

The possibilities are wide ranging and important. Scheduled expansion or year-end tax write-offs are one thing but purchasing know-how that could be licensed or acquiring an invention or patent to facilitate a major breakthrough is another matter. The answers to these questions can provide a source of leverage, help determine the objectives of the agreement, the amount to be paid, and may even be determinative of whether negotiations should proceed at all.

THE ROLE OF PERSONALITIES

Aside from motivations and objectives, there are always personalities involved. The opposing lawyer, the vice president for acquisitions, the comptroller, the technical people, the president, the board of directors, the stockholders... Each of these personalities will play a role in the ultimate outcome of the negotiation. Consequently, you will want to know who they are and how they are likely to act and react.

DON'T OVERLOOK THE NUTS AND BOLTS ISSUES

Finally, there are substantive issues relating to price, financing terms, transfer of assets, preservation of good will, and many others that must be addressed. These nuts and bolts issues form the heart of any agreement, and should be dealt with comprehensively based on a detailed assessment of all relevant circumstances.

SOURCES OF INFORMATION TO GIVE YOU A PLANNING EDGE

There is only so much information about the opposition that can be gleaned from prenegotiation phase. The rest will be revealed in the Opening Move and later stages. However, time should be allotted in your prenegotiation preparation to inquire into the opposition's motives, objectives, personalities and circumstances. Often your client can supply specific information or educated guesses on these subjects. Literature produced by your opponent such as annual reports, press releases, speeches by company executives are all potential sources of information as to their motivation for seeking a deal with your client. *Dun and Bradstreet, Standard & Poors* and *Moody's* all publish directories and maintain information services that can reveal much about a company's financial condition and holdings as well as the personalities and backgrounds of its executives. The *Wall Street Journal, Barron's, Forbes,* and *Fortune* are all sources for current business and financial news. Government announcements, congressional action, and pending legislation are additional sources of information. All of these should be scrutinized for clues as to motivations and objectives of the opponent and how the personalities of the opposition are likely to affect the conduct of the bargaining.

A DEAL IS SELDOM AS SIMPLE AS IT SEEMS

Anyone who has ever sold a tract of land to an unassuming, low-key buyer for a modest profit only to read later in the week about the plans for a new expressway or the location of an unexpected oil discovery on the very same piece of property can attest to the importance of sizing up the opposition.

Practical tip: A healthy sense of skepticism accompanied by persistence and the ability to look beyond the immediate aspects of any proposed deal will pay big dividends when it comes time to close.

MAKING THE MOST OF YOUR OPENING MOVE

Of the five primary functions of the Opening Move, there are three that should receive special attention. They are:

1. Information gathering
2. Identifying negotiation parameters, and
3. Initial use of leverage

WHY THE DIRECT APPROACH OF INFORMATION GATHERING IS ESSENTIAL

As mentioned previously, it is impossible to construct a final negotiation plan without sufficient information about the opposition. Sizing up the opposition prior to the Opening Move is certainly part of this process. However, in the great majority of all negotiations, only direct interchange between the parties can reveal the complete picture. If the opposition is experienced in negotiation theory and technique, you may never know the full story until the negotiation has been concluded, if then.

THE ELEVEN "MUST" QUESTIONS TO ASK IN A BUSINESS NEGOTIATION

In order to ascertain the information you will need, make sure you get answers to the following "must" questions.

1. Who has final negotiating authority?
2. What is the extent of that authority?
3. Are there any crucial points of procedure relative to your specific opponent or his industry of which you should be aware and understand?
4. Is there certain terminology or industry standards and practices of which you should be aware and understand?
5. Is the opposition sincerely interested in negotiating an agreement or is it using the process for other purposes such as a fishing expedition for information?
6. What does the opposition want in terms of Deal Points and Secondary Points?
7. What will they likely use as Trade Points?
8. What are their motivations, needs and the limits of their objectives?
9. What leverage does the other party possess?
10. What type of leverage will be most effective against the opposition?
11. What role will personalities play in the negotiation?

Answers or at least clues to these questions should furnish sufficient information to formulate a realistic approach to the negotiation. The problem lies in getting those answers. Techniques for doing this were discussed in Chapter Five, "Opening Moves."

THE ROLE HIDDEN FACTORS PLAY

Analysis of information will help identify the issues and ranges that comprise the parameters of the negotiation. A key point to remember when identifying the other party's primary and secondary objectives is that they are often just as likely to be based on purely personal or subjective considerations as on objective criteria. Ostensibly, all business agreements are concerned with objective criteria such as price, quality, or service and the like. However, for every objective criterion there is often a hidden subjective counterpart that figures into the final decision.

THE CASE OF THE JITTERY PURCHASING AGENT

For instance, assume a midlevel purchasing agent for a large corporation has the opportunity to buy a piece of business equipment from two different manufacturers, one of which is IBM and the other a solid, yet relatively new company. The products are comparable, but IBM is the more expensive of the two. Further assume that the purchasing agent is not totally secure in his position and is subject to criticism from his supervisor that can affect his career progress within the company. The purchasing agent finally decides to buy the IBM machine, citing the objective criteria that IBM has a proven track record and a reputation for quality products and service. The underlying subjective element is the fact that due to his insecurity, he opted for the more established and familiar company even though it cost more, knowing he could justify his decision to his superiors in the event something went wrong. The decision maker's job security played a role in the decision-making process.

THE MOST COMMON HIDDEN FACTORS

This is simply one example of the role hidden or concealed subjective factors play. Considerations involving power, prestige, ego, acceptance, job security, and personal prejudice enter into almost all negotiations to one extent or another. This is especially true in high-level business negotiations involving accomplished yet egocentric executives.

Practice tip: The information function of the opening move should seek to ascertain both objective and subjective considerations likely to affect the conduct of the bargaining. Though often not as apparent, hidden factors can often play a decisive role in the ultimate outcome of a business negotiation.

DEFINING PARAMETERS: DRAWING THE BOUNDARIES OF THE NEGOTIATION

Once information is gathered and analyzed, it's important to define the general parameters of the negotiation. This includes what the other party considers to be Deal Points and Secondary Objectives, as well as the degree of give and take that will be tolerated. Unlike lawsuit settlement negotiations which generally boil down to money, business negotiations are likely to have many more primary and secondary issues based on objective and subjective criteria. These points should be identified to the fullest extent possible before any concrete offer is made or accepted. This potential multiplicity of issues is another reason why the Opening Move is so critical.

THE PURSUERS AND PURSUED: WHICH SIDE ARE YOU ON?

Parties to a business negotiation can be placed in one of two categories: The Pursuer and the Pursued. The Pursuer is the initiator. He must first create interest in a deal if there is to be a deal. Once interest is established, the bargaining actually begins. On the other hand, the Pursued need only react to the overtures of the Pursuer. If the Pursuer fails to generate sufficient interest, the negotiation is over before it ever really begins. This differs from conflict resolution in that the alternative to lack of interest in a negotiated settlement is a lawsuit or a strike. The more merit in the plaintiff's position, the more interest the defendant is likely to have in a negotiated settlement.

GROUND RULES FOR REPRESENTING THE PURSUER

There are some basic ground rules to remember when representing a Pursuer.

1. *Create Interest*—This is your first objective. To be successful you must demonstrate how the deal will help the other party. This

generally means that the leverage of opportunity will be most beneficial. Sanction and uncertainty are to be avoided at this stage.

2. *Keep It Simple*—Getting bogged down in complex details at the outset is a sure way to kill any interest in a deal. Stress the major points of your proposition in straightforward, easy-to-understand language. Provide enough specifics to give the other side something to react to, but don't paint yourself into a corner by getting too specific on substantive points.

3. *Open High*—Once interest has been established, always open on the high end of the spectrum. An experienced negotiator will expect this provided you are not being totally unreasonable. As mentioned in previous chapters, this tack creates the trade points you will need for conducting an effective Give-to-Get negotiation. A common mistake of inexperienced law school graduates is to formulate a "fair" initial offer with no downward flexibility. This leaves you no room to retreat and depends totally on the good faith of the other party to accept your initial proposal. In all but the most exceptional situations, this is simply naive and ill-advised. An experienced business negotiator will be friendly, reassuring, and courteous when he informs you that his client just can't consider such an offer but would certainly be interested in a deal on substantially more advantageous terms. At this point, the lawyer who made the "fair" offer will swallow hard and turn slightly green realizing he must either withdraw altogether or begin to bargain trade points that he never intended to give up to ensure reciprocal concessions.

GROUND RULES FOR REPRESENTING THE PURSUED

The attorney for the Pursued business client always has the initial advantage. This advantage can be parlayed into a favorable conclusion provided he seizes this initial advantage.

Let the Pursuer do the talking: The more someone says, the more they are likely to reveal. The less you say, the less you are likely to reveal. By encouraging the Pursuer to elaborate and be more specific, the more valuable information you are likely to pick up. This knowledge can later be converted into powerful leverage.

Play it cool: Regardless of your level of interest and enthusiasm, you should never reveal it. If you are very interested and show it, you can count on this fact being reflected in the price your client will ultimately pay. If you have no interest and show it, you are likely to alienate or discourage the other side into abandoning the deal. The best approach is to be attentive, courteous, and noncommittal.

Control the timing and manner of your response: Blurting out your reactions in a meeting or over the phone can generally have more negative implications than positive. Patience and discipline will buy you the luxury of time to assess and analyze a proposal at your own pace. You are probably best advised to punctuate your response with some form of the leverage of uncertainty unless you are prepared to close the deal. Remember that the other side is scrutinizing your reaction in search of certainty and security. There is no reason to accommodate him unless, of course, it improves your position. If such is the case, do it.

Open low: The danger of creating an unreasonable floor is every bit as dangerous to the Pursued client as the trap of an unreasonable ceiling is to the Pursuer. Building in flexibility and creating trade points for the future is essential to the ultimate success of the negotiation.

NINE LEVERAGE TECHNIQUES TO HELP YOU TAKE CARE OF BUSINESS

All negotiations seek to change the status quo. In business this means creating an agreement or business relationship that didn't exist previously. The prime mover in altering the status quo is leverage. Of the four levers, sanction is probably the least effective, with opportunity being the most effective. The following represents nine examples of proven leverage techniques geared to business negotiation. They range from Machivellian sleight of hand to pure win-win tactics, all of which are reflective of the range of approaches that you are likely to use or encounter in the business arena.

CAPITALIZING ON TIME INVESTMENT

This is a commonly used technique related to the leverage of timing and uncertainty. It is particularly effective in helping forge an agreement with an opponent who has numerous alternatives and is not particularly committed to reaching an agreement with your client. The key is to get the opponent to expend a substantial amount of time in the bargaining process. In the event he begins leaning to an alternative offer, point out to him all of the time he has invested in the negotiation which would go for naught. This technique tends to make your offer a more attractive alternative to starting over on another deal which might or might not prove to be more advantageous than an agreement with your client.

Practice tip: In borderline situations, capitalizing on time investment can spell the difference between closing a deal and just coming close.

THE VANISHING OPPORTUNITY

This tactic combines the leverage of timing and opportunity. It involves offering a tangible incentive or opportunity in exchange for a quid pro quo. The trick is to link the offered opportunity to a specified deadline. This imposes time pressure requiring the opposition to act or suffer the consequences of the lost opportunity. Variations of the Vanishing Opportunity involve a tiered or structured withdrawal of the opportunity. For example, consider a seller's offer to finance an equipment purchase. Assuming the going rate is 11 percent, the seller's attorney offers the buyer financing at 10 percent if the deal is concluded within one week, 10.5 percent in two weeks, and 11 percent thereafter. This technique often helps spur an indecisive negotiator to action.

THE EXTERNAL DEADLINE

This approach involves creating or adopting a deadline for closing an agreement over which neither negotiator has any apparent control. The best example is setting an end of the fiscal year deadline for conclusion of an agreement, citing tax consequences as the reason for using this date. Regardless of whether the external deadline is really relevant to the transaction or is actually beyond the control of the parties, once you can convince the opposing party to accept it, half the battle is won. At·this point, the opposition will be required to take action. As deadline nears and the opportunity to pursue alternatives fades, your proposal becomes increasingly more appealing.

THE MASKED SANCTION

For reasons discussed earlier, the use of the leverage of sanction in the form of ultimatums or threats tends to be damaging to long-term relationships requiring good faith and mutuality. On the other hand, superior leverage of sanction is often effective in realizing short-run objectives. The "Masked Sanction" is designed to maximize short-term benefits without sacrificing long-term good will and rapport. As the latter half of the name implies, you deliver your demand and disclose the consequences to be suffered if the demand is not met. The only difference is that you tie the sanction to some force or circumstance beyond the control of your client. "If you don't accept our offer immediately, the bank will raise interest rates...the union will strike...the investors will withdraw...the stockholders will force our hand." In every instance, there is a sanction that will come from some independent source beyond your control.

Practice tip: Key phrases that can tip you to the Masked Sanction include: "It's out of our hands," "We don't like it either," "There is simply nothing we can do," "We'd like to, but...."

THE SNAG

This technique is often prefaced with an "Everything looks fine, but...." This variety of uncertainty is a method of injecting new problems or issues into the negotiation. The Snag is often used to sidetrack a negotiation which is not proceeding according to plan. By focusing on a particular problem or a new bargaining component, the parties are forced to shift emphasis from the previous negotiating agenda to a revised agenda set by you. This technique helps buy time. It also helps deemphasize troubling issues.

THE STRAW MAN

This is a technique of raising or injecting seemingly important, substantive issues into the negotiation which are in reality only trade points that can be used to extract concessions at a later point in the bargaining.

THE CRISIS

This is an application of uncertainty that seemingly puts the entire negotiation in jeopardy. It is often used in conjunction with communicating the Walk-Away Position as a possible alternative to negotiated agreement. The Crisis is a test of the other party's commitment to a negotiated conclusion. When used successfully, it tends to accelerate a final agreement.

SQUARE PEGS IN SQUARE HOLES

This technique involves a mutual application of the leverage of opportunity combined with a Give-to-Get personal negotiating style. For example, assume the buyer and seller are negotiating the sale of a parcel of land. The buyer's primary concern relates to financing, with price being a secondary concern. Conversely, the seller is primarily interested in getting the best price possible and would be willing to finance the transaction. By making the effort to identify each other's mutual concerns, an agreement becomes a reality through joint problem solving.

The key to this technique is to find as many issues as possible the parties can agree to or concede without substantially weakening their own position. This is nothing more than the leverage of opportunity being used to achieve win-win results. Unfortunately, it's not always that easy to find common ground, but when it is, the negotiators should make the most of it.

NEW WAYS TO SOLVE OLD PROBLEMS

This tactic utilizes creativity and innovation to develop new solutions to old problems. For instance, assume X wanted to purchase a slice of ice box pie from a local bakery but because of an allergy could not eat the crust. Additionally, because of strong feelings against wasting food, he refused to eat just the filling and throw away the crust. Further assume that all of the pies in the bakery contained crust. At this point, it would seem that there was an impasse that would preclude the transaction. Just as X was about to leave the bakery empty-handed, the proprietor devised a novel idea to facilitate the transaction. Instead of cutting the pie in the traditional style, he simply proposed that the pie be cut in such a manner so as to separate the pie filling from the crust. The proprietor promised to eat the crust since this was his favorite part of the pie. As a result X had his piece of pie without crust and without waste. The baker had his sale. Both were happy. The baker even charged a quarter extra for custom slicing the pie. A small price to pay for crustless pie and a valuable negotiating lesson.

THE SECONDARY NEGOTIATION: WHAT TO DO AFTER THE CLIENTS SAY YES

Another characteristic of business bargaining deals with what we refer to as the Secondary Negotiation. After the major points of a deal have been reached, there remains the task of drafting the final documents to be signed by the parties. At this point, the negotiation tends to focus on contractual language regarding everything from audit clauses, notice provisions, indemnification language, and numerous substantive and procedural details that clients tend to deem trivial and lawyers tend to deem crucial. More than one deal has been blown because of a failure to come to terms in the secondary negotiation phase.

Practice tip: Take responsibility for drafting the documents. The best technique for controlling the secondary negotiation is to assume responsibility for drafting the documents. This allows you to insert clauses and use specific language most favorable to your client. While you can count on the other lawyer to object to some of your clauses and language, he will likely accept much of it. In any event, the burden to react and object has been shifted to the opposition. The key to making this technique work for you is to be faithful to all major and minor points on which there has been expressed agreement. If the other lawyer suspects you of going back on what you have already agreed to, your draft will come under detailed scrutiny, not to mention the fact that you could be putting the entire deal in jeopardy. Once you have prepared the initial draft or proposed first draft, you should expect varying degrees of haggling over specific language. If you have previously established a good rapport, inspired trust, and conducted the negotiation with a minimal amount of personal animosity, you will likely find that your opponent will be less exacting on relatively minor points. On the other hand, a thorough lawyer will not approve anything that will prove detrimental to his client. As with other characteristics, some lawyers are simply more thorough than others. Act accordingly.

HOW TO HANDLE THE CLOSING

Because of the long-term implications of business negotiation, it is important that the negotiation be concluded on an upbeat note. Even if you have the leverage to push the other party into a one-sided agreement, if the agreement depends on future good faith and reciprocity in performance, you are probably heading for trouble. One must have an incentive to make a deal work. That incentive can be either economic or personal, or both. For instance, assume parties X and Y enter into a contract whereby both stand to gain. However, during the negotiation of that agreement, X's lawyer was abusive and rude to both Y and his attorney. The personal bitterness engendered by the lawyer will, at least to some degree, carry over to the performance of the contract. Y will be much quicker to find fault with X's performance or be much more likely to settle the score at some later date. This is unfortunate but avoidable.

In light of the importance of maintaining personal relationships, the following points relative to closing a business agreement should be kept in mind.

SEVEN KEYS TO A SUCCESSFUL BUSINESS CLOSING

1. Don't overreach, even if you have the leverage and skills to do so.
2. Never make the opposing attorney look bad in his client's eyes.
3. Allow the opposition to make concessions gracefully.
4. Downplay your successes and emphasize the other parties' victories.
5. Provide the opposition the ability to save face by making apparent concessions that can be magnified.
6. Repair any personal damage done during the conclusion of the negotiation. A word of praise for the opposing attorney's profes-

sionalism and integrity or ability to handle a difficult situation will go a long way to negate any problems created during the negotiation. The same is true as to the opposing client.

7. Stress the positive and mutual aspects of the deal.

WHAT TO DO WHEN FACED WITH A LOSING BOTTOM LINE

All of the foregoing points assume you and your client emerge from the negotiations on the long end of the stick. If, on the other hand, you find yourself at a disadvantage shortly before closing, analyze the deal carefully and objectively with your client. If the negotiated agreement will not put you in a more advantageous position, you are best advised to invoke your Walk-Away Position or at least indicate that possibility so you might gain a few last-minute concessions. As we have stated previously, there is never any magic in a deal for the sake of a deal. If you don't stand to gain from the proposed transaction, say no.

13

Negotiating Lawsuit Settlements

15

Negotiating
Lawsuit Settlements

To most people, the trial lawyer is a personification of the glamor and excitement of the legal profession. Because of the mass media, everyone just naturally assumes that all litigators are courtroom crusaders who tirelessly pursue justice at every turn with an irresistible combination of quick wits and silver tongues. It's the best of Perry Mason and Clarence Darrow all rolled into one.

Actually, trial lawyers spend the overwhelming part of their time interviewing clients, drafting pleadings, taking depositions, and researching legal issues. Most of their courtroom work involves arguing motions or making routine appearances at hearings. The relatively few cases they actually do try are usually far from dramatic. In the final analysis, more than 95 percent of matters in litigation are settled through negotiation. To put it another way, the average trial lawyer uses his negotiation skills about twenty times more often than his trial skills to resolve litigated conflicts.

THE FIRST STEP TO MASTERING LAWSUIT NEGOTIATION

As in the area of business negotiation, there are special considerations, patterns, and rules regarding negotiation theory and practice that apply only to lawsuit settlements. An understanding and appreciation of this special body of knowledge is the first step to improving your skills in this specialized area of negotiation.

EVERYONE HAS SOMETHING TO GAIN IN BUSINESS

As we have seen, business negotiators are optimistic by nature. Everyone has something to gain from striking a deal. Theoretically and often in practice, there need be no losers in a business negotiation. This is why the Win–Win approach is so often emphasized by negotiation theorists and one important reason we stress its use in the business arena. At worst, failure to reach agreement will usually only result in a lost opportunity and unproductive expenditure of time.

EVERYONE IS A POTENTIAL
LOSER IN A LAWSUIT

By contrast, in the usual litigation settlement agreement everyone has something to lose. For the defendant, the measure of loss is obvious. He faces the dilemma of having to pay the plaintiff to withdraw his claim via settlement or risk the alternative of having to potentially pay more in the form of an adverse judgment. A victory for the defendant is preservation of the status quo often at the expense of substantial counsel fees and court costs.

Less obvious, but just as real, is the risk borne by the plaintiff. At best, the unsuccessful plaintiff loses in terms of time spent in pursuit of a fruitless claim. At worst, the plaintiff can suddenly find himself exposed to liability by virtue of a counterclaim filed by the defendant's attorney. More than one seemingly "can't miss" plaintiff's case has been transformed into a voluntarily nonsuit in the wink of an eye by a well-timed counterclaim.

Emotionally, both the plaintiff and defendant are losers. Every lawsuit exacts a toll in terms of anxiety, pressure, animosity and stress. No one is immune. Even the so-called detached professionals such as trial lawyers, insurance adjusters, and corporate officers who profess that litigation is just part of business find themselves falling victim to the psychological toll exacted by litigation.

WHY WIN–WIN LOSES ITS LUSTER IN SETTLEMENT BARGAINING

Because everybody involved in a lawsuit has something to lose—except, ironically, the defense attorney, who is usually paid by the hour—it's easy to understand why the Win–Win approach isn't suited to litigation-oriented negotiation. However, this is not the only reason why the Win–Win approach is often unrealistic in resolving litigated disputes.

As mentioned earlier, a positive approach is necessary to preserve and enhance important personal relationships and to ensure the long-term mutuality and reciprocity needed to make contracts work. In lawsuit negotiation, these reasons for utilizing a positive, less combative approach are not present. In most instances, personal relationships are badly strained or permanently destroyed by the time lawyers become involved. Additionally, there are few if any long-term considerations regarding reciprocity and mutuality. Once litigation becomes an option, there is little worth saving. At this point, the plaintiff is usually trying to salvage his position with a monetary recovery to compensate him for what he has already lost. Because the courts are involved, defendants, unlike their business counterparts, don't have the luxury of sitting tight in the face of a lawsuit. They must do something or risk having a default judgment entered against them. As a result, the tone, style, and approach used in a lawsuit negotiation can differ dramatically from other types of bargaining. In order to succeed, you must understand and appreciate what is required in terms of strategy, tactics, and personal style.

UNNECESSARY HARDBALL TACTICS CAN SPELL TROUBLE

All of this is not to suggest that Hardball is the only negotiating style that will work in settlement bargaining. Far from it. More than one plaintiff's lawyer has made a bad situation worse by employing unnecessary hardball tactics against a seemingly helpless defendant. Always keep in mind that a smart defense lawyer with little or no leverage can still make life miserable for the plaintiff and his attorney if given reason to. This can range from looking a "little harder" for a counterclaim, to working the opposition into the ground by means of prolonged discovery, or making maximum use of dilatory tactics that can extract a harsh cost in terms of the time the plaintiff must wait to get his money.

Practice tip: As mentioned in previous chapters, our advice is to ignore a doctrinaire approach and do what is most effective. This may mean using Give-to-Get, Hardball, or even Softball tactics. The watchword is flexibility, combined with a recognition of the factors that make lawsuit negotiation a far different exercise than other, more positive types of bargaining.

USING THE LEVERAGE OF UNCERTAINTY AND TIME

The key to understanding what makes a lawsuit settlement negotiation tick can be summed up in two words: uncertainty and time. Generally, both plaintiffs and defendants will always be seeking to substitute certainty for uncertainty. A plaintiff will often forego the uncertain possibility of recovering a $100,000 judgment for the certainty of a $20,000 settlement. In addition to sure money, the plaintiff has also avoided the uncertainty that a jury could return a verdict of zero against the plaintiff. On the other side of the table, the defendant who pays the $20,000 settlement has reduced his potential loss by 80 percent and has bought the certainty and peace of mind that goes with a dismissal of a complaint with prejudice.

Besides certainty, the parties to a settlement recognize the relationship of time and money. Even if the plaintiff has a good chance of recovering a $100,000 judgment, he must weigh the time factor that must be assigned to discovery, trial, and a probable appeal by the defendant. Even where liability and damages could be proven, all of these factors could delay the actual receipt of the money by years. Consequently, plaintiffs are usually much more willing to trade money for time.

Practice tip: The effective negotiator who understands the importance of uncertainty and time is in a much stronger position to use these two levers to effect more favorable settlements for his clients.

PREPARING FOR A LAWSUIT NEGOTIATION

Despite the pressure and stress associated with lawsuit negotiation, this type of bargaining is generally much more manageable from the standpoint of preparation than the usual business negotiation. The primary reason relates to the relative simplicity of issues involved. In most cases, the primary issue is money. For instance, in personal injury negotiations between a plaintiff's attorney and the insurance company which has been subrogated to the claim, the primary issue relates to how much, if anything, the plaintiff's claim is worth. Consequently, the entire negotiation hinges on questions of liability, extent of injuries, and the plaintiff's ability to prove his case. The likelihood and amount of settlement will be determined by the strength of the plaintiff's case based on these few factors.

On the other hand, the normal business negotiation tends to be much more complex in terms of issues and other factors affecting the deal. To illustrate, consider the common situation in which a company is negotiating to acquire a smaller competitor. There are a multiplicity of issues involved. Besides the bottom-line purchase price, the parties must deal with the identification and valuation of assets, financing terms, the status of and transfer of outstanding supply contracts, employment agreements, trademarks and trade secrets. There are also issues relating to liability for previous and prospective debts and defaults as well as tax, securities, and antitrust implications of the transaction.

This is not to say that lawsuit negotiation will always be necessarily less complex than contract negotiation. High-stakes business litigation involving a deal gone sour can take weeks, months, and even years of negotiation to resolve. However, under most circumstances, lawsuit negotiation involves fewer and more simplified issues.

HOW YOU CAN BENEFIT FROM THE PREDICTABILITY OF YOUR OPPONENT

Just as the subject matter in lawsuit negotiation can often be simpler than other types of bargaining, the plaintiff's ability to predict the other side's actions and responses can be maximized with a greater degree of accuracy. This is especially true in cases involving insurance carriers. Every insurance company has its own internal rules, procedures, and unconscious habits. The totality of these characteristics and patterns make up the company's operating profile. Some companies tend to emphasize more heavily resolution of claims through settlement than other hard-line companies who prefer taking their chances in court. Knowing the attitude of the insurance company toward settlement can play a major role in your preparation for negotiation. For instance, when dealing with a hard-line company, why waste your time with elaborate settlement overtures that will more than likely fall on deaf ears? Filing your lawsuit and pressing your case will probably be the only thing that will persuade this type of company to negotiate.

IN-HOUSE RULES AND GUIDELINES ARE KEYS
TO PREDICTABILITY

Beyond a company's general reputation, there are certain in-house rules of thumb or formulas that are used to guide their adjusters and legal counsel in settling claims. For instance, in certain companies, a junior adjuster will have authorization to settle claims up to a certain amount, without receiving approval from a supervisor. Once that level has been reached, the supervisor becomes involved. After a certain point, which is generally once suit has been filed by the plaintiff, local counsel will be brought in to handle the negotiation. Insurance company employees, as well as the company's retained counsel, are bound by the philosophy and internal procedure of the client's company. The more a plaintiff's attorney knows about the workings of a given company, the more effective he can be in adopting an effective negotiation strategy.

HOW TO READ A COMPANY'S OPERATING PROFILE

An example of reading a company's operating profile is illustrated by the company that never makes a settlement offer until suit is filed and discovery begun. When dealing with this type of company, your knowledge of their patterns will lead you to the obvious conclusion that pressing for an early settlement would be useless. As a result, you can use your time more effectively on other matters while waiting to push for a settlement after discovery, when it is likely to be accepted. This is just one example of how insight into a company or law firm's operating procedure can pay off.

Practice tip: Knowing and understanding the general and specific aspects of a company's operating profile is an important part of your preparation phase. Being privy to internal information will give you an edge when planning your negotiating strategy and tactics.

THE BEST WAY TO FIND OUT IS TO ASK

The best way to find out about a company or law firm's operating procedure if you have had no prior dealing with them is to ask other lawyers. Most plaintiff's bars have developed an unofficial "book" on each major insurance company and insurance defense firm in their locality. As would be expected, the defense lawyers generally do a pretty thorough job of researching and cataloging the traits, patterns, and habits of the plaintiff's lawyers. Regardless of which side you find yourself on, you should always make a point of tapping this source of information when dealing with a company or lawyer with which you are unfamiliar. This type of information can often play a deciding role in the outcome of a particular settlement negotiation.

KEEP THEM GUESSING: DON'T FALL VICTIM TO PREDICTABILITY

As with most aspects relating to negotiation, the dangers of predictability can cut two ways. Uncovering the internal procedures of the opposition is not enough. To be successful, it is essential that you not be predictable. This means avoiding unconscious patterns and habits. Always try to keep the opposition guessing as to what moves you will make or how you will react to a certain maneuver or tactic. Even the cleverest move loses its effectiveness if everybody knows it's coming. Keeping the opposition guessing is your best insurance against ineffectiveness.

UNDERSTANDING THE DEFENDANT'S NATURAL EDGE

In lawsuit negotiation, the defendant always starts with an edge. To some, this may sound strange, especially in situations in which both the law and facts appear to be on the side of the plaintiff. Nevertheless, it's true. The primary reason relates to the burden of changing the status quo, which is squarely on the plaintiff. This requires the plaintiff to initiate every aspect of a suit whether it involves filing a complaint or actually proving the case in court. Only when it appears the plaintiff will be successful will the defendant be in a frame of mind to pursue settlement negotiations seriously. This natural edge greatly affects the way plaintiffs and defendants approach lawsuit negotiation.

THE BARRIER DEFENSE
AND HOW TO OVERCOME IT

In a lawsuit settlement negotiation the goal of any plaintiff's lawyer is to convince the defendant that paying less to the plaintiff now will be better than paying more at a later date. To do this, the plaintiff must contantly press the lawsuit forward so as to exert maximum pressure on the defendant. The defense lawyer, seeking to maintain the status quo, counters by erecting as many barriers between the plaintiff's and defendant's bank account as possible. When the plaintiff hurdles one obstacle, the defendant merely falls back to the next barrier, knowing all the while that time is running and that the plaintiff's energy and resources are being tested. Experienced defense lawyers know that anyone can file a lawsuit but that few have the energy, commitment, or ability to push the case to a final litigated conclusion. The road from demand letter to an executed judgment is exceedingly long and perilous. A plaintiff has ample opportunity to stumble. Defense motions, counterclaims, depositions, and interrogatories can all be used for the dual purpose of exposing the weaknesses in plaintiff's case and consuming time to preserve the status quo. In many instances, the plaintiff may withdraw or abandon the case for any number of reasons, ranging from an unsuccessful bluff to simply running out of steam. Even if the plaintiff is successful at one stage, there will always be another barrier to hurdle. The following chart illustrates the "Barrier Theory of Defense" in a typical personal injury case.

Plaintiff's Action	Defendant's Likely Response
1. Demand letter	1. Ignore/deny liability/make accusations
2. File complaint	2. File answer: general denial/counterclaim
3. Deposition	3. Take additional depositions of plaintiff
4. Interrogatories	4. Counter with interrogatories to plaintiff
5. Motions	5. Counter motions
6. Jury trial	6. Neutralize plaintiff's case
7. Jury verdict	7. Appeal

PATIENCE AND PREPARATION: THE TWO KEYS TO HURDLING THE BARRIER DEFENSE

Experienced defense attorneys know that time is one of their best friends. It erodes the enthusiasm and resolve of most plaintiffs and many of their attorneys. Consequently, they are in no hurry to negotiate. Defense attorneys will only enter into serious negotiations once they are convinced that the plaintiff intends to go the distance and that their case is strong enough to create sufficient uncertainty as to what the outcome would be if the plaintiffs did pursue the claim to trial.

PATIENCE IS A MUST

Patience on the part of the plaintiff's attorney and his client are absolutely essential to the success of any lawsuit negotiation strategy. This is difficult for plaintiff's attorneys, especially when they are acting pursuant to a contingency fee arrangement. But it is harder still for the client who has had little or no experience with the judicial process. The seemingly endless delay has been cause of disillusionment for more than a few plaintiffs who had a meritorious claim. If you represent the plaintiff, you should take steps as early as the initial conference to lower the client's expectations and engender a sense of patience.

Practice tip: One way of doing this is to explain to the client how the process works and what he can expect from the opposition.

A realistic appraisal of the time considerations involved will help both you and your client determine the commitment each has toward pursuing the case. It's much less painful to decide on the front end that you aren't prepared in terms of time or resources to see the case to a conclusion. Making this decision early can save months of money and effort.

HOW TO USE PREPARATION TO OFFSET THE DEFENDANT'S ADVANTAGE

Preparation is the other key to forcing the defendant into a settlement frame of mind. The plaintiff's preparation starts with a thorough investigation of the strength and value of the case. For instance, if the case is strong in terms of liability but weak in terms of damages, it makes no sense to mount a major effort to obtain only a nominal settlement. Substantial proof problems or circumstances that would indicate a successful counterclaim are other factors that could color the advisibility of pursuing the claim in the first place. Attorneys who squander hundreds of hours a year on marginal cases that yield only token settlements can only blame themselves for their lack of bottom-line success. Plaintiff's lawyers would do well to remember that they earn their fee when they close files, not when they open them.

Once the decision to accept the case has been made, it's vitally important to build the strongest case possible. Experienced defense lawyers are not easily intimidated. Too many young attorneys waste valuable time making threats and drafting half-baked complaints based on cursory investigation and haphazard preparation. Their time would be much better spent documenting the evidence needed to establish and prove each element of their lawsuit. As stated previously, only when a defense lawyer is convinced of your credibility, commitment, and the merits of your case will he move toward serious negotiation.

PLACING A REALISTIC VALUE ON YOUR CLIENT'S CLAIM

Assuming there is probable or at least arguable liability, the true task for the plaintiff's lawyer in settlement negotiation is to place a realistic value on his client's claim. You can rest assured that the defendant is doing the same. Determining the value of a claim is especially important in cases involving insurance.

Insurance companies are in the business of resolving claims. Some companies favor delay and ultimate litigation, while others favor settlements. However, when faced with a situation in which liability is clear or highly probable, almost every company will want to settle. This is especially true in light of cases that have held insurance carriers liable to their policy holders for acting in bad faith in not settling meritorious claims. When liability is clear or highly probable, the question is not whether to settle but only for how much.

There are numerous factors that go into placing a dollar-and-cents value on a claim. The factors are essentially the same for both parties. While the following list is not meant to be exhaustive, it does provide a checklist of factors that you will want to consider when evaluating a case. Add to this list any additional specific information, local guidelines, or customs that might be applicable:

FOURTEEN POINTS TO CONSIDER WHEN VALUING A CLAIM

- Presence or absence of insurance
- Policy limits
- Other resources or assets of defendant
- Possibility of defendant receiving indemnity or contribution from others
- Verdict expectancy as to subject matter and locality
- Settlement patterns of plaintiff and defendant
- Time value of money to plaintiff and defendant
- Experience, reputation and credibility of plaintiff and defense counsel
- Ability of plaintiff to prove liability
- Extent of plaintiff's special and general damages
- Ability of plaintiff to prove damages
- Presence or absence of external and internal deadlines or schedules
- Aggravating or mitigating factors; emotional factors
- Any other specific relevant factors or circumstances

Both the plaintiff and defendant will spend the bulk of their prelitigation investigation and much of the discovery process trying to find the answers to these specific questions. Neither party should make or accept any substantive settlement offer until this information is compiled and analyzed. Above all, when conducting this inquiry, it is absolutely necessary that the parties be as objective and realistic as possible. To illustrate the dangers of being overly optimistic or haphazard in the investigatory phase, consider the case of Mrs. Hurt and her son, Ime.

THE HURTS AND LAWYER GREEDY: WHAT NOT TO DO

The Hurts were involved in an automobile accident with a car driven by Joe Sloshed. Prior to the accident, Sloshed, who had a reputation of being a heavy drinker, had a couple of beers at a bar. According to the Hurts and other witnesses, Sloshed ran a red light, lost control of his car, and slammed into the Hurt's automobile, which was parked in front of their house. Mrs. Hurt and her son suffered minor cuts and abrasions but miraculously escaped injury.

Neither was treated by a doctor. The police determined that Sloshed was not intoxicated at the time of the accident. After telling all of this to Lawyer Greedy, the attorney ascertained that Sloshed was covered by Mutual of Everywhere Insurance Company and that he carried a $200,000 liability policy. Greedy, who is a teetotaler, has a very strong personal prejudice against drivers who drink. After hearing the Hurts' story, he expressed outrage at what had happened and assured them he would teach Sloshed and his insurance company a lesson. Based on the foregoing information, Greedy filed a $750,000 lawsuit on behalf of the Hurts. After a thorough investigation that included extensive discovery, the insurance company admitted liability and offered $3000 to settle the case. The Hurts were insulted, feeling they were due a large settlement based on the circumstances surrounding the case and assurances their lawyer had given them. Greedy promptly turned the offer down, feeling that the prospect of a lawsuit together with the admissions of liability and aggravating circumstances would result in a substantial settlement offer. The big offer never materialized. The case went to trial on the issue of damages only. Since liability had been admitted, the judge excluded all evidence relating to the circumstances surrounding the accident, ruling that it was irrelevant. The jury returned a verdict of $700 for Mrs. Hurt and $250 for Ime. Greedy, who was working on a 40 percent contingency, received $380 for six months' work. The Hurts went away full of resentment against the legal system, the defendant in general, and Lawyer Greedy in particular. Unfortunately, all of this could have been avoided had Greedy done his homework, maintained his perspective, and not made wild, unsubstantiated promises to his clients.

SOURCES OF INFORMATION
FOR ASSESSING YOUR CASE—
AND YOUR OPPONENT'S

Assuming you have resolved to be as objective and realistic as possible, the next step to putting a value on your claim involves gathering the information you will need to assess the strength of your case and your opponent. The logical starting place is with your client. As we have stressed in previous chapters, and suggested in the preceding example, you must make every effort to be thorough and professionally skeptical while at the same time showing compassion and support for your client. This can be a difficult balancing act. After you have interviewed your client, reduce his account of the facts to writing and submit it to him for his approval. This procedure requires him to consider and approve each detail he has given you.

Practice tip: This is an effective technique for weeding out exaggeration and getting to the truth before making accusations and demands. After interviewing your client, confirm his or her story with other witnesses. You must first convince yourself that the claim has a reasonable chance of success, otherwise you may be on the road to nowhere.

Even the most thorough investigation will not give you all the information you need to assess the questions of liability and damages fully. At this point, you must marshal all of your experience and resources to fill in the missing pieces. This is where an evaluation of the reputation, habits, and settlement patterns of the defendant, the experience and reputation of the opposing attorney, and other such information will come into play. Discovery is another fruitful avenue when it comes to uncovering specific facts and circumstances relating to the case. Finally, the opening moves of the negotiation itself will provide a great deal of valuable information.

THE OPENING MOVE: CAT AND MOUSE GO FISHING

Experienced plaintiff and defense attorneys often use the Opening Move to launch fishing expeditions for information in the classic tradition of a game of "Cat and Mouse." The following conversation is fairly typical:

Plaintiff's Attorney: "Well, Steve, I'd like to get together with you and resolve this accident claim we're handling which involves your insured."

Adjuster: "What about it?"

Attorney: "You've seen the file. It's obvious you're man ran the stop sign. It really just gets down to damages."

Adjuster: "From your version of the facts, it might be obvious. But our investigation indicates that liability is not as open and shut as you would have us believe."

Attorney: "Well, let's put that aside for now. I'm primarily interested in what your company would be willing to dispose of this claim for."

Adjuster: "Well, I'm not sure we are going to make an offer. However, it would be helpful to know what your people are looking for. That would at least give me some idea of whether there is even any sense in pursuing this."

Attorney: "You've got a copy of my complaint. We're asking the court to award $750,000."

Adjuster: "Sure, now what do you really want?"

Attorney: "All I can get, you know that. However, I would imagine my client would be willing to take the policy limit less an amount to avoid having to try it."

Adjuster: "And what would that be?"

Attorney: "Well, I couldn't tell you until I confirmed the policy limit."

Adjuster: "That's confidential."

Attorney: "You know I can find out in discovery."

Adjuster: "Well, I think the limit is $200,000, but I'd have to check. Assuming it was, how much would your client be looking for?"

Attorney: "I'll tell you what, let me put the pen to paper and get back to you."

This type of conversation takes place thousands of times a day across the country. Here, both parties were sparring for little bits of information to help them assess how the other side viewed the strength of the claim. In this situation, both the plaintiff and insurance carrier know that in the usual case the policy limits set an absolute ceiling amount on settlement expectancy. Consequently, they both know that in most cases the actual settlement amount will be substantially lower. In this particular situation, the adjuster wanted the attorney to know that the actual policy limits were lower than the plaintiff thought them to be. Rather than just saying so, the two felt compelled to play Cat and Mouse.

Practice tip: If possible, you should try to get the opposition to quote a settlement figure. This often gives direct information as to how seriously the other side considers the plaintiff's claim to be. The higher the figure, the more seriously the insurance company regards the claim.

SUBSTANTIATING YOUR CLAIM

Both plaintiff and defendant tread a fine line with regard to how much and what kind of information each is willing to reveal about the case. Generally each side will try to establish the strength of his particular position hoping to persuade the other side to reevaluate the case. The telephone is one method; correspondence is another. As mentioned earlier, a primary function of the demand letter is to substantiate the claim by providing your opponent with information that will lead him to the conclusion that both you and your client's claim is credible. A well-written demand or response letter can provide subtle information that will help you substantiate your position. You should refer to the chapter on correspondence and apply the principles dealing with the uses of correspondence to substantiate your position.

FINDING THE SETTLEMENT RANGE

Once the defendant has been persuaded to negotiate, and preliminary values have been assigned to the claim, the key to reaching agreement is finding a settlement range. This involves plaintiff and defendant reaching a broad consensus as to the value of the claim. If the plaintiff's and defendant's general evaluations fall within the limits set by the other, a settlement range is defined and an agreement becomes a probability. For instance, assume the plaintiff in a personal injury case is seeking damages of $100,000. He is willing to accept as little as $12,000 but feels the claim is realistically worth $27,000. On the other hand, assume the defendant is convinced that the plaintiff has a strong case on liability with arguable damages. It is willing to pay up to $15,000 while feeling that the plaintiff might accept as little as $3000. Consequently, a primary and secondary settlement range is established as in the following illustration.

The area of overlap between the defendant's high ($15,000) and the plaintiff's low ($12,000) creates the primary settlement range. This has the effect of narrowing the official stated differences

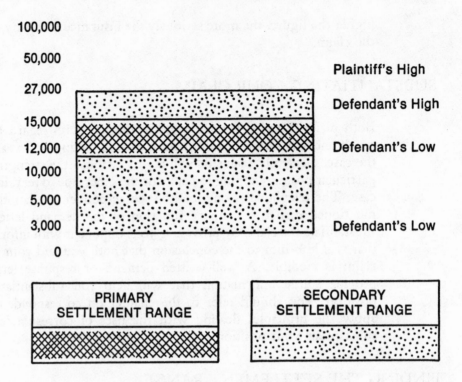

between the parties from $100,000 and $0 to $15,000 and $12,000. The final settlement will most likely fall between $15,000 and $12,000.

Besides the primary range, a secondary range of $27,000 to $3000 is also established. Provided one or both of the parties redefine or adjust their high and low positions, the settlement could fall within this range. Depending on the amount of leverage and the effectiveness of the parties in using it, the various highs and lows of the parties will fluctuate accordingly. The end result will either be an agreement or the Walk-Away Alternative of a trial. Of course, even if one of the parties walks away from the negotiation, the process of redefining the value of the claim can and often is renewed at some point prior to a jury verdict and in some instances even subsequent to a judgment pending an appeal.

Failure to achieve a settlement range will usually result in a continuation of the litigation process until a settlement range can be established or a verdict is rendered. To illustrate, assume the plaintiff's low figure was $15,000 and defendant's high figure was $10,000.

Based on these assumptions, the settlement range chart would appear as follows:

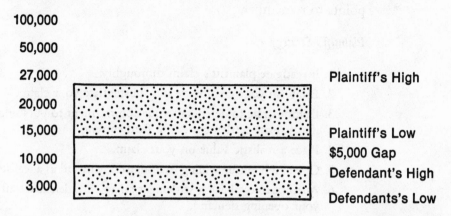

100,000	
50,000	
27,000	Plaintiff's High
20,000	
15,000	Plaintiff's Low
10,000	$5,000 Gap
3,000	Defendant's High
	Defendants's Low

Here, there is no overlap thus no settlement range. A $5000 gap exists. As a result, the litigation process would continue until either the plaintiff adjusted his low figure downward or the defendant raised his high figure.

In the usual case, as the trial date nears, uncertainty becomes more acute, and the threat of sanction more pronounced. As a result, the parties often find that matters previously thought to be non-negotiable or firm suddenly become subject to compromise and reevaluation.

THE ROLE OF THE COURT AS A THIRD PARTY

An additional factor when litigation is imminent is the court. Judges often assume the role of a catalyst to the resolution of the dispute. The judge's role can range from that of a mediator to a hardsell third party.

In extreme instances, the high and low acceptable settlement figures are subject to reevaluation even as the trial proceeds. A poor performance by a witness, revelation of surprise facts, or an evaluation of how the jury is perceiving the testimony can prompt one of the parties to reevaluate their positions.

Practice tip: In any event, attorneys should always remember that settlement is always an option up to and in some cases, even after a verdict is returned.

While there is no such thing as a foolproof blueprint for conducting a successful lawsuit negotiation, there are some basic points to remember.

Plaintiff's Strategy

1. Investigate plaintiff's claim thoroughly.
2. Establish your credibility and substantiate your claim.
3. Demonstrate to defendant your commitment to pursuing a verdict if a realistic settlement is not forthcoming.
4. Place a realistic value on your claim.
5. Open high but be willing to readjust downward in a realistic manner.
6. Attempt to establish a settlement range with defendant after making your opening demand.
7. Persist in your efforts to close the gap but always be prepared to resume the litigation process if an acceptable settlement is not forthcoming within a reasonable time.

Defendant's Strategy

1. Make the plaintiff initiate action.
2. Use the barrier defense and agree to negotiate only if you believe the plaintiff will continue to press the claim and has a strong possibility of success.
3. Investigate the claim thoroughly.
4. Place a realistic value on plaintiff's claim.
5. Open low but be willing to adjust upward in a realistic manner.
6. Attempt to establish a settlement range with plaintiff after making your opening response to plaintiff's demand.
7. Persist in your efforts to reach a fair settlement remembering that you have the advantage of the barrier defense.

THREE MORE FUNDAMENTALS FOR SUCCESSFUL SETTLEMENTS

Beyond the foregoing considerations, both parties should observe the following points:

ALWAYS LEAVE THE DOOR OPEN

Even if you feel you enjoy a leverage advantage you should never burn your bridges. Things can change in a hurry. New facts, unexpected witnesses, an unfavorable jury are just a few of the innumerable things that can go against you.

TALK IN RANGES

The pitfalls of the floor/ceiling trap in business bargaining are equally applicable to lawsuit negotiation. Once the discussion gets around to concrete settlement offers, it's best to talk in terms of ranges rather than fixed sums, "We're looking for $10,000 to $15,000" gives you some maneuvering room. "We want $12,000" does not.

USE THE CLIENT AS A HEDGE

When discussing settlement ranges, or offers, use the client to hedge. This is simply an application of limited authority. "I'm not sure the plaintiff will accept $12,000. I'll recommend it but I can't make any promises." First of all, the ultimate settlement decision always rests with the client. Second, the approach gives you an out if the client will in fact not accept $12,000 or if there are other reasons to reevaluate the offer.

CLOSING CONSIDERATIONS: NEVER ASSUME THERE WILL BE A SETTLEMENT— AND NEVER ASSUME A SETTLEMENT CANNOT BE REACHED

No matter how close the parties are to a settlement, the litigation process continues until an agreement is reached, papers are signed by the parties, and the judge signs the order of dismissal. Never assume there will be a settlement. Practical experience leads us to the conclusion that you should always be prepared to proceed with the suit up until the final order of dismissal. Often lawyers banking on a settlement tend to abandon preparation for trial only to be faced with a collapse of talks. This results in losing points at trial or being forced to make costly and unnecessary concessions to salvage an agreement to dismiss.

Because uncertainty heightens as the trial date deadline draws closer, chances are that your best opportunity for settlement will come at the eleventh hour even though it appears that the parties are hopelessly deadlocked. This is why it is essential for you as the attorney to maintain your level of preparation, keep your poise, and never assume that an agreement cannot be reached. By following this procedure, chances are that you will accomplish settlements you did not think possible. However, if the settlement fails to materialize you will be ready to proceed to the Walk-Away Alternative of a trial.

THERE WILL ALWAYS BE ANOTHER LAWSUIT

If you are a trial lawyer, you can bank on the fact that there will always be another lawsuit involving a previous adversary. This means that no matter what happens in the short run, there are long-term considerations to think about. As mentioned in previous chapters, our advice is to keep it professional no matter what the outcome. Your ability to conduct settlement negotiations with professionalism is essential to your long-range credibility and effectiveness.

CONCLUSION

As we stated at the outset, much of what has been presented in this book is neither new nor radically different from what successful people have been doing for years. We are also the first to echo the common refrain that many of the principles and concepts dealt with in this book are based on common sense. These are precisely the reasons why the material in this book is of value to you.

Our primary objective has been to apply these principles to the context of a law practice in the simplest, most direct manner possible. This is not a book just to be read; it is a reference to be used. If you will take the time to understand and apply these principles, concepts, tactics, and ploys to the files you handle everyday, we are confident that your ability to achieve results for your clients will be enhanced in less time and with less effort. In a word, you will be a better lawyer. In the final analysis that's what we're all trying to accomplish. Here's to your success.

Index